HAUNTED OBJECTS OF PENNSYLVANIA

BY ED KELEMEN

Published in The United States of America

2021 Nemeleke Publishing
New Florence, PA

CREDITS

The illustrations in this book are the work of the author who has either taken and modified the picture himself or acquired it from public domain, then modified it from the original for this book.

Some of the events and stories in his book have been included in other publications by the author, but have been modified so as to select only that part that suits the subject matter of this publication. They have appeared in *Pennsylvania's Haunted Route 30, Paranormal PA, Haunted Route 22, Weird West Overton,* and *Pennsylvania's Haunted Churches and Cemeteries.*

Linda Ciletti has again produced an incomparable cover. Visit with her on Face Book for a chance to see additional examples of her wonderful work.

TABLE OF CONTENTS

TABLE OF CONTENTS
(Continued)

WHAT IS A GHOST?

WHY ARE THEY HERE?

Some other words for ghost are: apparition, bogie, familiar, spirit, haunt, hant, haint, materialization, phantasm, phantom, poltergeist, shade, shadow, specter, spook, sprite, vision, visitants, and wraith, to name a few. These names are interesting, but they don't tell us *what* a ghost is. For that, we'll need to look elsewhere.

Let's look at Merriam Webster's definition of a ghost. It says that a ghost is a disembodied soul; ESPECIALLY the soul of a dead person believed to be an inhabitant of the unseen world or to appear to the living in bodily likeness. The word comes from the Middle English word *gost* or *gast*, and from the Old High German word *giest*. Its first known use was before the 12th century.

Over the last few decades, medical science has determined that we are in essence, a bit of electrical energy. That everything that makes us who we are is contained within our central nervous system and network of neurons which is similar in operation to a high-powered computer. Similar, but *different.* Similar in that computers imitate brain function as far as data input and output, storage, processing, and programming. Different in that brains function both electrically and chemically, are self- aware, have feelings, and have personality. There are a myriad of other ways that brains differ from computers.

Here's one big way they differ: The greatest scientific minds in the world *know* how a computer works; they only have *theories* about how the brain works. Those neurons I mentioned earlier are only 15% of the cellular make-up of the brain. 85% of the cells are called *glia* and nobody seems to know what they do, but they have something to do with learning, memory and repair.

So, we come full circle to our belief that a person's essence cannot be destroyed. It's just an extension of the law of the conservation of matter that says matter cannot be destroyed, it can only be transferred into something else, such as energy.

Our physical body is only a vessel to contain our essence, or soul, if you will. Upon the demise of that body, the non-physical part of a person departs that body and lives on, sometimes to cross over into another plane of existence, and sometimes to stay on in this plane for one reason or another.

Those of us who consider that death is simply a transition and not an end consider a ghost to be nothing more than the continuation of a living person's essence after his or her corporeal body has ceased to function. *"Ceased to function" - isn't that a nice way of saying died?*

Ghosts are just people like you and I. And like people, ghosts have many personalities, moods, and character traits. Some are nice, some are average, and some are nasty. There are times they want to be left alone and there are times when they are a bit more gregarious and are willing to interact. And, just like people, I've found that treating ghosts with respect gets their respect in return. Remember the magic words: *please* and *thank you.*

Why are they here on the corporeal plane of existence? Why haven't they transitioned to the next plane of existence, the afterlife, Heaven, Valhalla, Hades, the Elysian fields, Loka, the Happy Hunting Grounds, or whatever you chose to call it?

Because, for one reason or another, they have unfinished business here. Perhaps they have a compelling message to deliver to someone who is important to them. Sometimes a person has suffered such a violent, trauma-filled death that they don't even know they have passed on.

Some are satisfied with existence on this side and have decided they don't *want* to cross over. They're having fun *here*, so why go *there*? The ghosts of children are often in this category.

Some feel that their life on the earthly plane has been less than exemplary and are resisting crossing over lest they wind up in an overly warm place. Hell, Tartaros, Naraka, and Gehenna come to mind.

Some are being held here against their will, after running afoul of other denizens of the dark, one of the greatest reasons to avoid playing with Ouija Boards.

Sometimes loved ones such as parents, grand parents, spouses, and care-givers feel as though someone they have left behind here on the physical plane still need their love and caring. They linger on to make sure that those they love and care for will be able to make it on their own. Once they feel assured, then they will go to the light that welcomes them into the next level of existence, the spiritual one.

And finally, there are those timid souls who find themselves stuck in a sort of limbo, no longer part of this worldly existence, but afraid to cross over into the ethereal one. They are fearful of going to the light and either don't know, or can't feel their loved ones already there waiting for them.

HAUNTED OBJECTS

Sometimes, for one reason or another, a spirit becomes inextricably attached to an inanimate object. And, wherever that object goes, so goes the spirit.

Why is that? Usually because the object has some extreme measure of importance to the spirit from his or her days of corporeal existence. The spirit resides within or close to that object, identifies with it, and will not let it go, such as in the following examples:

A rich girl had a wedding gown of unbelievable beauty and opulence designed and crafted for her wedding that never took pace. In death she gets the opportunity to do that which she was denied in life – to preen and strut in that fabulous gown, turning first this way, then that way, knowing that, at last, she is the most beautiful woman in the assemblage. And now she cherishes this moment for eternity.

Grandma spent her twilight years gently rocking in her favorite chair at the living room window watching the seasons change in the neighborhood where she has reared her children and doted over her grandchildren. Rather than spend her afterlife in some place that, although serene and comfortable, she'd rather stay here where so much love has been present during her earthly existence.

Other spirits stay behind not so much to try to catch memories of love and grandeur as to make a statement. Such is the case with the young Irish lad who has left his indelible mark upon a jail cell wall in the form of a bloody hand print that will never be eradicated until his wrongful execution is reversed.

Other items recall days of celebration in the form of musical instruments that, to this day, still provide the occasional listener with a form of spectral entertainment of past performances recreated by often unseen players.

Extreme trauma sometimes captures the essence of an event in the form of a haunting. Such as ambulances used to transport the horrifically injured and dying from accidental and other means to hospitals and morgues.

Sometimes an individual has experienced the depth of despair causing him, or her, to take their own life. And their anguished visage looks out over the happy, healthy outer world from the glass of the window where they are trapped until they can be convinced that there is a better way and they can escape their curse and cross over.

There are nearly as many reasons for an item to be infused with the spirit of a departed one as there are such items. But they all have one thing in common – extreme or long-lasting emotions. These emotions run the gamut from love to hate to despair and even to happiness and everything in between.

But what happens to some of these items? Grandma's rocker gets donated to a thrift shop. A cauldron used to boil the flesh from an individual's bones winds up in an historical society's collection. A radio that plays by itself for the enjoyment of spirits is sold off when the motel where it was located is liquidated.

Often persons will be attracted to one thing or another, say at an antique or resale store, flea market, or yard sale. They buy it, take it home, and then begin to experience unusual events within their home. That's because Granny will still rock, her unseeing eyes gazing over a landscape that is no longer there, the trapped spirit will continue to gaze from its mirror over the shoulder of the hapless man trying to remove the stubble from his neck and chin with that incredibly sharp razor, and that toy doll that was such a bargain at the thrift store has a mind of its own, moving itself to where it prefers to be rather than the location that was picked for it.

Read on...

PART I

ROCKERS HOBBY HORSES AND CRADLES

HAUNTED ROCKER AT THE JEAN BONNET TAVERN

Intersection of Routes 30 and 31
Bedford, PA

The Jean Bonnet Tavern has a wonderfully rich and diverse history, starting as an unnamed French fort in the early1700s. General Forbes rested at the location in 1758 while building the Forbes Road en route to defeating the French at Fort Duquesne, which was later renamed Pittsburgh. During 1794, George Washington and his troops camped here while on their way to quelling the Whiskey Rebellion.

The inn and tavern date to 1762 when the

land was purchased by Robert Callander who built the solid stone structure that still stands there today. Jean Bonnet bought the property in 1779 and, since then it has changed hands multiple times serving as an inn, tavern, restaurant, and private residence. Nowadays, it is a fantastic restaurant, tavern, and bed and breakfast. In a separate log building is its gift shop, famous for the quality and selection of its items.

With all this history and the number of people who have passed through during the last two-and-a-half centuries the Jean Bonnet has been a place where extreme emotions have been experienced. There is a report of General Forbes hanging a captured spy on the premises, a young lady is supposed to have committed suicide there in the early 20th century, and 200 years of hard-drinkers have populated the establishment. All of these have left a lasting impression on the place in the form of spirit activity.

The Rocking Chair

One of these spirits has claimed a rocking chair in the upstairs middle room for her own. The rocking chair sits by the window. People who have stayed overnight there say that they were just sitting on the bed admiring the room when, for no reason whatsoever, the chair began slowly rocking.

To a person, those who have witnessed this activity report that they have gotten the impression that the spirit is of a woman, gently rocking the chair while looking out the window.

Nobody knows who she is, or what her personal history involves. She is probably attached to the chair and not the inn and will leave with the chair if its is ever removed from the building.

EMMA YOUNG'S ROCKER

Alfred's Victorian Restaurant
38 North Union Street
Middletown, PA 17057

Situated just five minutes from Harrisburg International Airport in an 1888 Brownstone Mansion, Alfred's Victorian is a discerning restaurant featuring entrees from the Tuscany area of Italy, as well as dishes originating in America and other European countries. The elegance of the furnishings is matched by the exquisite menu. Popular with everyone, it is especially popular with couples looking for an intimate romantic setting because of the way certain tables are made private with strategically-placed screens.

The mansion was the home of Simon Cameron Young, a banker and descendant of Senator and Abraham Lincoln's Secretary of War Simon Cameron. He bought it in 1902 and lived t here until his death in 1933 with his wife, Mary Emma Young.

Emma lived on there as the matron of the house until her death in 1948. In her afterlife, Emma has stayed on in the mansion maintaining her position of Lady of the House. She has been frequently seen in the house by employees and visitors alike. She was even photographed by one of the owners who was taking a group picture of the restaurant's staff. She probably insisted on being in the photo since she considers herself the supervisor of all things in the mansion she has called home for nearly 20 years.

She isn't shy about making herself known. Her rocking chair announces her presence when its runners noisily come into contact with the hardwood floors when she gets agitated.

So, if while you are enjoying an aperitif at your table you hear the unmistakable sound of hardwood runners interacting with hardwood flooring, it is just Emma indicating her dissatisfaction with something or someone on the premises.

My mother always took pains to place a throw rug under the runners of the rocking chair in our home so as to not have the hardwood floor scratched by them. I'm just commenting.

HALLWAY ROCKER AT

The Inn at Phillips Mill
2590 River Road
New Hope, PA 18938

The Inn at Phillips Mill is located in an 18th century refurbished stone barn featuring French cuisine under the watchful eyes of two renown chefs.

Dining in the winter months is beside a cheery crackling fire. In the warmer months, you can choose to sup outside on the patio surrounded by in-season flowers. As inns go, it is small, having only 5 rooms to let. But these five rooms are as upscale as the menu featuring comfortably furnished, romantic rooms perfect for a weekend getaway.

As you sit descend the stairs from the second floor you may be one of the patrons who have the experience of being ever so slightly jostled by the passage of a dignified, definitely upper class grande dame as she passes by on her way up. You just won't be able to see her right now.

Since you won't be able to see her on her way up, how do we know what she looks like? That's because she has been seen in the second floor hallway as an apparition wearing a long, narrow waisted, high collared gown of the type fashionable during the late 1800s.

Other times she takes a break and is seen sitting demurely in the rocking chair conveniently located there for her. If you want, when she isn't using it, you may rock a bit there as well. Just be ready to vacate that seat if you feel an unearthly cold hand on your shoulder.

GRANNY'S ROCKING CHAIR

Butler County, PA

While at a book signing, I met a gentleman who told me the following story. It illustrates the fact that extraordinary things happen to everyday people.

"I'm from Butler County here in PA and have been for all my life. Same with my wife. Let me tell you something that happened a few years ago.

"It was in the late 1990s or thereabout and my wife's momma had taken ill, so we went over to

10

her house a lot to care for her. One particular day I had worked all day cutting firewood and was just about completely out of energy.

"Well, you see, her mom lived in the old family home on the family farm that had been in the family for generations. It went back to before the Civil War. It was a big ole two story frame thing with add-ons and covered porches and all.

"That particular day when I was dog tired, we went over to help out as best we could and make her mom comfortable and bring her some food. If I remember right, she had a touch of some kind of flu or something. Anyhow, while the missus was upstairs tending to her mom, I decided to relax on the couch downstairs. I think I had the TV on, but I don't remember that for sure.

"I must've drifted off to sleep, cause the next thing I knew, I was woke up by the sound of the old rocking chair creaking back and forth on the wood floor over by the front window.

"I rubbed my eyes and looked over there and saw a really old lady just rockin' back and forth, back and forth, smiling and looking out the window. She was wearing a dress with an apron and a little cloth covering her hair.

"I called over to her to see if I could help her or something and, right before my eyes, she disappeared, just like that! She looked at me,

11

smiled and faded away.

"I ran upstairs to my wife and mother-in-law and told them all about it.

"They told me not to worry about it, it was my wife's grandmother's favorite chair and she still likes to rock away in it from time-to-time."

MOM'S PORCH ROCKER

The Inn, Farmhouse, and Brewery at Turkey Hill
991 Central Road
Bloomsburg, PA 17815

The Inn, Farmhouse, and Brewery at Turkey Hill sits on a knoll that is the top of Turkey Hill. The farmhouse has been there since Martin Van Buren was President of the United States. The year was 1839. The other buildings came later. Since 1984, it has been operated as a B & B. Additional dining options are available there as well. The brewery offers casual dining and craft beers in a rustic setting while fine dining is available at the Farmhouse Restaurant.

13

The area around the complex offers many things to do and see, ranging from hiking to kayaking, shopping, art galleries, theater, and treasure troves of antiques. When you are done with all the activities you have planned, return to the Inn, put your feet up and relax. The Inn is conducive to relaxation since it is a wonderfully serene establishment with gardens, patios and quiet walkways to explore.

One of the places you may choose to just kick back and relax may be the glass-enclosed porch at the Inn, offering you the opportunity to enjoy an unobstructed view of the outdoors from a climate-controlled environment that is air conditioned during the hot months and heated during the cold ones.

While you are there, you may be joined by what some people have said is the ghost of the mother of one of the owners. She, although not being visible on her forays to the porch, will take up residence in her favorite wooden rocking chair and will rock to-and-fro in it, its runners creaking on the solid floor while not a single breath of air is available to help it move.

CAPTAIN VICARY'S PORCH ROCKER

The Captain William Vicary Mansion
1235 Third Avenue
Freedom, PA

Sitting high above the street on Third Avenue, overlooking the multiple tracks of the huge Conway railroad switching yard on the Ohio River is the Captain William Vicary Mansion. Built over a period of three years, it was completed in 1829 and was the home of this War of 1812 Naval hero until his death in 1842.

The beautiful structure, made of locally-quarried sandstone watched as the town of Freedom evolved from a company town erected to support the needs of Jonathan Betz and Stephen Phillips' steamboat building business. It quickly grew and supported a steam engine building business, a gristmill and distillery, three hotels, and two doctors.

The dowager continued to watch over the town as the steamboat business waned in the mid-1800s to be replaced by railroads. The next town upstream on the Ohio River, Conway, PA became the location of the world's largest switching yard and even today is the home of Norfolk Southern Railway's huge freight switching yard. And the Vicary Mansion stopped watching the Ohio River being plied by steamboats. Instead it spent its days and nights watching millions upon millions of tons of freight being shuttled, shifted, and switched into and out of the freight yard 24 hours a day, 365 days a year.

In the mid-1960s PA Route 65 was about to be modernized and widened to accommodate the increase in road traffic that rendered the old route obsolete. Part of that modernization was to be the condemnation, demolition, and removal of this grand old lady who has witnessed a century and a half of progress and change from the old steamboat days to the heyday of the railroad, and now the age of the automobile.

The citizens of the area would have none of that and a grassroots campaign resulted in the purchase and restoration of the mansion by Beaver

County who now leases it to the Beaver County Historical Research and Landmarks Foundation. It was placed on the National Register of Historic Places in 1974. Saved from the wrecking ball, the building is now a museum depicting a historic house of a unique type made from locally quarried sandstone by the skilled masons of the mid-1800s.

Along with over 150 years of historical significance, a couple of specters were also saved from that wrecking ball. It seems as though Captain Vicary has never left his beloved home. He still watches over river, rail, and road traffic from his vantage point above Third Avenue. Reports have filtered down that the electric chandeliers which replaced the gas lights in the mansion's downstairs rooms now turn on and off with no corporeal assistance and these same chandeliers swing back and forth on their chains with assistance from neither breezes nor human hands.

Phantom voices are heard conversing in the next room from where you are, even when those rooms are unoccupied. Perhaps it is the retired sea captain still arguing with the craftsmen who originally built the mansion, even after all these years. After all, that argument resulted in a Supreme Court decision in 1842 to settle that disagreement. Since that decision wasn't rendered until shortly after his death that year, maybe he argues on still.

He also allows his presence be known via the proliferation of cold spots throughout the mansion. Cold spots come and go depending on what room he decides to inhabit at any given time.

Sitting on the front porch of the mansion, facing and overlooking the railroad switching yards is a wooden rocker. The rocker's province is unknown. It may not even be an antique. Nevertheless, someone, possibly Captain Vicary himself, basks in the warmth of summer sunsets sitting in that rocking chair contemplating the passage of time and the march of history from that vantage point while slowly the chair rocks back and forth, back and forth, unaided by a visible human presence.

THE ROCKING HORSE

Archbishop Pendergast High School
403 North Lansdown Ave.
Drexel Hill, PA 19026

Archbishop Pendergast High School, originally an all-girls facility merged with all-boys Monsignor Bonner High School in 2006 making the institution a coed facility. This was just the latest incarnation of the historic site which has been reborn many times since an unusual octagonal mansion was built on 37 acres of this high ground in 1850 by Christopher Fallon for his family. Named

"Runnymede" after the family's ancestral home in Roscommon County, Ireland it was sold to Colonel Drexel 32 years later and became a famous residence in Drexel Hill, which is named after the colonel's family.

Runnymede was the first building in the county to be lit with gas lamps which may have contributed to the disastrous fire that occurred in 1908. That fire burned the landmark mansion to the ground leaving only the gatehouse standing.

The remaining building and the surrounding acreage was allowed to lie fallow for the next nine years until the Roman Catholic Diocese of Philadelphia purchased it as a site for St. Vincent's orphanage. It was run by the Sisters of Charity and was designed to hold 500 orphans. 125,000 people attended the dedication of the orphanage on May 9, 1920. For the next 32 years, orphaned children were taken care of at the location.

However, by 1953 the number of orphans had diminished to the point where the facility was much too large for the population of orphans. The remaining orphans were transferred to a smaller facility while the existing building was re-purposed into a Catholic High School for boys named for Archbishop Pendergast.

A couple of years later, in 1956, a new building was constructed nearby that became the Monsignor Bonner High School for boys and the Archbishop Pendergast High School was classified for girls only.

And this brings us up-to-date as of 2006.

During these 170 years of existence the area and most particularly, the school building has picked up its fair share of haunts and folk lore, particularly from its years as an orphanage.

There are many stories about otherworldly happenings here.

One tells of a nun who supposedly hanged herself in the bell tower, which her spirit still haunts. The bell tolls unaided from time-to-time and her image appears in one of the openings of the tower. There have been reports of children running through the halls late at night arguing and fighting. And an unseen group of young girls is heard laughing, giggling, and talking. From the conversation that these young spirits engage in it has been learned that one of them is named Lily.

A couple of the rooms dating back to its days as an orphanage have yet to be remodeled into new classrooms and are used for storage. One of these rooms is a focal point of paranormal activity. Dusty old furniture skitters hither and non with no earthly assistance that can be observed, and leaving no track in the dust of the floor,

One of the items in this room is a venerable, if not antique, rocking horse. If anyone remains in the room for an extended period of time, the rocking horse will start rocking of its own volition. One explanation that has been put forth is that it is the spirit of a murderous orphan who died in the orphanage of a freak accident. I don't know why the spirit is called murderous, since there is no history of a murder ever occurring at the place throughout its many incarnations.

Personally, I like to believe that it is a happy spirit of one of the orphans who is reliving the happy time he or she had as a child playing in the rocking horse now that it doesn't have to be shared with as many as 500 other children.

WHO ROCKS THE CRADLE?

The Jennie Wade House
548 Baltimore Street
Gettysburg, PA

Virginia Wade was the only civilian killed by hostile fire during the battle of Gettysburg. She was but 20 years old. She actually moved from her home on Breckenridge Street a few blocks away to her sister's home to avoid the battle and to assist her sister, Georgia, who gave birth a few days earlier. She was known as Gin or Ginnie to her family and friends. She got the appellation of Jennie as a result of a typographical error in a newspaper and it has stuck ever since.

At the time, Jennie was betrothed to Johnston Hastings Skelley, known as Jack to friends. He was a corporal in the 87th Pennsylvania Volunteers, a regiment that saw action in numerous Civil War Battles. Unbeknownst to Jennie, Jack had been wounded at the battle of Winchester, Virginia that had run from June 13 to June 15. He died from those wounds on July 12, 1863.

On July 3, 1863 Jennie was kneading dough for loaves of bread that she and her mother had been baking for the Union soldiers who were fighting to keep possession of the town.

It has been said that she was overheard commenting, "If anyone in this house has to die this day, let it me me."

At about 8:00 am the morning of July 1, 1863 a Confederate soldier in the top floor of a house not too far away fired his rifle at the house, adding its presence to the other 150-plus bullet holes in the house.

However, this particular bullet, a Minie ball, passed through the kitchen door, then the parlor door before striking Jennie in her left shoulder blade and continuing on through her heart before exiting her body into her corset. She died instantly, falling to the floor.

Jack Skelley, lying in a field hospital some 80 miles away never learned of the death of his fiance.

But, separated by war, the two lovers were joined in death. Jennie and Jack are buried near each other in the Evergreen Cemetery on Baltimore Street, just three blocks from where she died.

Because of the intensity of the battle that raged around the building during those days in July, 1863, the Jennie Wade house is indeed haunted. There have been uncounted reports of paranormal activity within its walls ranging from orbs to apparitions and items moving on their own.

Because Jennie and her beau died within weeks of each other, they were unable to carry out their plans for a wedding. It is said that Jennie doesn't want other women to suffer the same fate as she did. So, it has been claimed that if female visitors place their finger in the interior door's bullet hole, then Jennie will give them a special gift—they will receive a marriage proposal within a year.

As I mentioned before, Jennie's sister gave birth shortly before the battle ensued and she dutifully did what she could to help her sister with the young one. I can only imagine what it must have been like to care for a new born while a battle raged about.

She probably rocked little Lewis in his cradle perhaps singing softly to him to help him sleep in those first tumultuous days of his life. And, she has continued to do so ever since.

The sturdy brick house where the McClellan family lived during the 1860s, and where Jennie died has become known as the Jennie Wade House and is operated as a shrine and museum dedicated to her memory.

Tours of the authentically furnished home are conducted daily and it is frequently the location of paranormal activity. Psychic/medium Beverly LaGorga was on one of those tours a few years back with her husband and young son.

During the tour, the guide pointed out an antique wooden cradle that dated back to approximately the time of the Battle of Gettysburg and mentioned that Jennie probably tended to her baby nephew who reposed in just such a cradle.

Suddenly, with no earthly assistance, the cradle started rocking slowly back and forth, back and forth at just the speed one would imagine was needed to lull an infant to sleep.

Transfixed, Beverly watched the cradle until it slowed and stopped rocking after a period of one to two minutes. Perhaps the ghostly baby sitter had satisfied herself that the baby was sleeping and went about performing some other chore while he slept.

In any case, Beverly eventually caught up with the rest of the tour and left the building, the memory of the ghostly babysitter tending the child forever etched into her memory.

PART II

MIRRORS

WHY MIRRORS?

In my investigations into haunted objects throughout the state, mirrors have frequently turned up as having a spiritual attachments of one kind or another. They are one of the most common objects found to have this otherworldly affinity. And they have a rich history concerning this.

Stories about haunted mirrors abound throughout history in every place on the planet. So, it is no coincidence that folk lore is rife with stories about them.

Here are some of them:

The ability to suck out souls. In order to contravene this ability of mirrors, they are removed from any room where there is a gravely ill or dying person. That's because people in a weakened state are more vulnerable to the negative power of a mirror.

To look into a mirror at night by the illumination provided by a candle is to invite demons and malevolent spirits to come across into the dimension of the living. Some believe that you may even experience a presentiment of death, even your own, by doing this.

In certain areas of Central and Eastern Europe precautions are taken to turn mirrors so that they face the wall in any room where a person has died. If that isn't practical, then the mirror is covered with a blanket or something else that blocks light from entering the mirror. Failure to follow this protocol may result in the deceased's essence being sucked into the mirror, or even being transformed into a vampire.

Another bit of lore has it that a mirror should never be positioned in a bedroom where it can reflect a person's bed as this can allow negative energy to enter the sleeping person's psyche causing nightmares. If a mirror is so placed, one protection is to cover it when the bed is used for sleeping.

Mirrors should be frequently moved so that they don't spend too much time in any one location. This is to prevent them from becoming portals between the worlds of the living and the dead.

Mirrors that have solid backings and are allowed to stay in one place for extended periods of time can become portals between the land of the living and the land of the dead. See the previous notation. *(Personally, I would tend to think that the solid backing would prevent the transference between the different planes of existence by providing a barrier.)*

Vampires do not have reflections in mirrors, anyone who has seen movies about Dracula and his ilk knows that. But how many people know that the reason for that is that the reflecting ability of mirrors is caused by a thin silver coating on the back of the glass to create a mirror? And that silver is an anathema to vampires? So, does that mean that modern coatings like Mylar *do* actually reflect vampires? It would sure make it easier for them to shave.

And, finally, mirrors have the ability to harbor spirits, showing them as reflections when a person looks into the mirror. These frequently appear as faces behind the reflection of a person looking into the mirror. Other times, they appear as smoke or mist. This is the haunting of mirrors that happens most frequently and the one that we are most familiar with.

Throughout Pennsylvania there are stories about mirrors harboring spirits, most often in the form of residual hauntings, possibly because mirrors can sometimes act as a psychic batteries, storing psychic energy.

This section gives many examples of this.

BACK BAR AT

The Iola Hotel
Millville, PA

Millville is a small borough in Columbia County, covering a tad less than one square mile and consisting of a little less than one thousand residents. Although settled in 1792, it wasn't incorporated until 1892, its growth hampered by lack of access. It wasn't until 1887, when a railroad line was constructed through the little town allowing passenger and freight travel in and out of the community that it began to thrive. There was an earlier growth spurt after 1856 when a road finally found its way into the town allowing easy transport to and from Bloomsburg on the bank of the Susquehanna River ten miles to the south.

In order to serve people arriving and departing on that railroad, the Iola Hotel was constructed in 1900 along what is now PA Route 42. This unprepossessing two-story frame building holding a tavern, restaurant, and hotel served the people of Millville at that location for over one hundred years. Just like any building open to the public for that long, it has picked up quite a bit of psychic activity.

Shadowy entities appearing to be wearing long flowing black dresses were encountered upstairs where the hotel rooms are located. They were observed entering rooms and walking around corners.

Downstairs in the tavern area, seats on the bar stools spin on their own, with no earthly assistance whatsoever.

Patrons sitting on the bar stools that front the bar in the tavern have pretty much no choice other than to study the huge mirror that is the back bar facing them from a few feet away. That way they can verify whether their hair needs combed, their attire straightened, or a bit of food wiped from their chin. They can even offer a toast to their reflection when the mood strikes them. Imagine their surprise

when, while looking into that mirror, they see people other than themselves looking back at them. People who haven't been in the bar for a century. People sporting high-backed, Victorian-style collars and hairdos. People who aren't there when the patron turns around to see who is behind him wearing such unusual clothing in this day and age.

The observance of these spirits in the mirror happened so many times that it is highly unlikely that they have their origin in the spirituous drinks the patrons partake of whilst perching on those bar stools.

Should you wish to visit this haunted location, you will be disappointed. As of this writing the establishment is closed with the building and property for sale.

GRANDMOTHER'S POWDER ROOM

1806 Uniques & Antiques
1454 W. Pitt Street
Jennerstown, PA 15547

As you proceed westward on the Historic Lincoln Highway, also called US Route 30, you will enter a quaint little village named after the discoverer of the Smallpox Vaccine, Edward Jenner. Originally called Laurel Hill, Jennerstown was named after him in appreciation of his vaccine that helped eliminate the disease of smallpox which had devastated the countryside with virulent outbreaks, particularly among young children.

On your left as you enter town is a large white-painted brick building that loudly proclaims with huge letters on one side, "1806." It is the home of 1806 Uniques and Antiques, a one-of-a-kind warren of treasure troves where you can find anything from a 2000 Beatles poster to a repair kit for early 20th century typewriters and everything in between. The "1806" refers to the year the building was built by The Butt family, who operated it as both a home, a stage coach stop, and an inn.

The building has been continuously occupied since the day it was built and has seen various incarnations.

For a period of time during the 1800s, it was used as a courthouse for a local squire who had his office on the second floor. Local miscreants accused of crime ranging from public drunkenness to murder found themselves pleading their cases in front of the squire's desk before being sent to the county jail in Somerset twelve miles to the south.

Local lore has it that there was a trap door on the floor to accommodate an indoors gallows where those sentenced to death would be sent to have an interview with their maker before being admitted as a citizen of the nether region known as hell.

It is even suspected, although not verified, of being a stop on the Underground Railroad.

The new owners, a mother and daughters team have had many paranormal experiences and encounters within the building since they took over in 2016/.

Numerous Paranormal Investigative groups have visited the premises and documented a variety of both active and residual hauntings in the building,

One spirit in particular makes her presence known in and near the second floor powder room. She is an elderly lady wearing a light blue dress covered by a floor-length white apron. She has been seen as a full-body apparition just outside the powder room door and in the hallway adjacent to it by at least six different people.

However, she has been seen most often inside the powder room when someone looks into the mirror there. That's when she appears as a reflection in the mirror, most often looking over the shoulder of the person peering into the mirror.

Fran, one of the owners, was describing this

spirit to a previous owner and occupant of the historic building and that person replied, "Oh my God! That's my Grandmother!"

THE BACK BAR MIRROR

The Spotlight Lounge
1400 Washington Blvd.
McKeesport, PA

In 1891, about 500 residents on a bluff outside the City of McKeesport, PA got together and decided to form the new Borough of Portvue. The original consensus was to name it Grandview because of the "Grand" view it had overlooking the city of McKeesport and the confluence of the Youghiogheny and Monongahela Rivers. Somehow or another, probably because McKeesport had the word "port" as part of its name, they decided to call it Portvue. And that's the name it was incorporated with in 1892.

The little borough prospered and was settled by steel workers, coal miners and other hard-working, middle class folk, eventually growing to a population of around 5,000 by the mid 20th century.

Infrastructure in the borough was needed to serve these people, and general stores, pharmacies, gas stations, and auto repair shops sprung up to handle this. One of these businesses is the Spotlight Lounge opening its doors in a small brick one- story building during 1951 as a neighborhood watering hole and gathering place.

Unfortunately, the borough fell upon hard times. The steel mills all but closed, the mines shut down and people left by the hundreds. The borough is now home to less than half of its peak population and the Spotlight Lounge has suffered along with it. Its glory days are behind it, but it is still going strong and people still like to go there for the friendly service and intimate setting.

And, some people have never left, even after passing way. Their spirits live on at the bar. Or, more precisely, within the mirror of the bar.

People sitting at the bar have looked up from their conversation to see old friends' and acquaintances' reflections in the mirror across from them. Usually people they haven't seen in quite some time. Spinning around on their bar stool they greet their old friend and offer to buy them a drink. And they discover nobody there standing behind them. That's when they remember that particular friend they just saw is deceased.

His, or her mortal remains have long since been committed to the earth, but their essence lives on within the mirror, perhaps longing to join in the camaraderie and festivities of years gone by.

ONE ANGRY MIRROR

Ligonier, PA

A middle-aged gentleman, obviously in great health and physical condition, along with his wife who also obviously partakes of the healthy lifestyle bought both of my books about the hauntings along Pennsylvania roadways: *Pennsylvania's Haunted Route 30* and *Pennsylvania's Haunted Route 22.*

Thumbing through the book about Route 30, he commented, "I see you missed one."'

That piqued my interest, so I asked' "How so?"

Here's what he told me -

Right off Route 30 in the Ligonier area was a house that dated all the way back to the 1830s. It was in such a deteriorated condition that it couldn't be restored and was scheduled for demolition.

On a particularly sweltering August afternoon he noticed the workmen preparing the site, so he asked the supervisor wearing the white hard hat if he could look around.

"No skin off my nose," was the reply. He took this as tacit permission, so he and his wife went on in.

Picking their way through the first floor

rubble, they were amazed to find a lot of the contents still in place. But most of the items were just old, not antique, and in such a state of disrepair as to be only fit for kindling wood. It looked like squatters had been living in the house for some time. But the intrepid pair of "diggers" persevered, examining all the nooks and crannies they could find. Eventually that doggedness paid off when a closet yielded treasure.

Treasure to them, that is. To anybody else it was just a filigreed and gilded old mirror showing the patina of age. And dust, lots of dust.

"Honey, this mirror would be perfect for over the table in our foyer," she exclaimed.

He agreed. It fit the style of the old table in the entrance-way of their home and was the perfect size as well.

Sneezing in the cloud he created by blowing the dust layer from some of the filigreed decorations., he commented, "It'll go perfectly with that statue of Dad's that we put on that table."

Right here I interrupted his story to ask why he had a statue of his dad in the foyer.

He explained that it was a statue that had previously *belonged* to his dad, not a statue *of* his dad. That point cleared up, he continued.

He picked the mirror up and removed it from

the closet. Suddenly the temperature dropped enough to give both of them a chill.

"Honey, let's get out of here," his wife demanded.

The old house was then filled with the sounds of doors and windows slamming shut.

He grabbed the mirror and they headed for the door which was now closed. They had to struggle with it to open it.

"Looks like the mirror doesn't want to leave its home," he quipped.

But they took the mirror away anyway, cleaned it, and gave it its place of honor in the foyer. But it brought with it a sense of foreboding and suspense. It looked great, but it made them uneasy whenever they looked into it.

"It's kind of hard to explain," he said. "It was always as though an unseen someone was looking over my shoulder when I looked into it, An unseen someone who bore me ill will. And I wasn't the only one who felt that way."

They decided that, even though the mirror fit so well into the foyer decor, it had to go. They decided to only keep it until they could find a replacement.

The mirror must have sensed their intentions because one day shortly after they made their decision about it. it "fell" from its place on the wall. As it fell, it struck the statue, cleaving the head from it as neatly as a guillotine. But the mirror survived the "fall" without damage, not even scuffing the gilt.

They waited no longer and got rid of it immediately by donating it to a church-based resale shop where, they hoped, its anger would be dissuaded.

If you come across an obviously antique mirror at a church bargain basement resale shop, oval in shape and about three feet tall with filigreed gold leaf flowers all around the frame, be wary about giving it a new home in your home.

ROOM 6

The Logan Inn
New Hope, PA 18938

This historic inn is one of America's oldest continuously-operating inns having been in operation since 1722, ten years *before* George Washington was born. During its first five years, it was run as a tavern only, but began offering overnight lodgings in 1727. Located mid-way between Philadelphia and Easton on the Delaware River it is ideally situated to serve both the traveling public and local customers. Its reputation for fine dining and luxury accommodations has spread far and wide during these nearly three centuries of existence. It is currently under renovation that will add 100 rooms to the original 16 when completed in Spring of 2020.

Hopefully the addition of rooms and modernity to the original structure won't interfere with its well-deserved reputation as one of the most haunted hostelries in the Northeastern United States.

Shortly after World War II, during a street fair in 1946, a psychic named Parker Dehn encountered a screaming, crying child on the premises while conducting a session in the Inn's parking lot. Audience members also heard the wailing child, but could not locate the origin of the noise.

This extraordinary occurrence repeated itself the following day, then stopped when the street fair concluded, only to re-emerge again the following year during the fair.

Elsewhere in the inn, a Revolutionary War soldier roams, visiting the bar, the dining room and the basement. It is thought that he is the spirit of one of the soldiers whose bodies were kept in a makeshift morgue in that basement during the war.

The shades of children and adults wander about the inn and windows have been known to throw themselves open with no earthly assistance during those hours of the night between 2 AM and 4 AM when anything can, and usually does, happen.

Inside the inn a number of spirits have taken up residence with Room Number 6 being the most haunted. The spirit of a former owner's mother is spending her afterlife there. She usually announces her presence with the smell of lavender perfume wafting on the air.

The bathroom in Room Number 6 has a conveniently-placed mirror over the sink, just as in countless other hotels, motels, hostels, and B&Bs throughout the world. The difference with this one is that it is haunted. Haunted by spirits who have to share the looking glass

A number of people who were either using the mirror to shave, comb their hair, or brush their teeth have said that they saw the visage of a man standing behind them looking over their shoulder making eye contact with them.

Other have seen the shades of two young children staring back at them from inside the mirror. Nothing much is known about these kids, it is assumed that they are the spirits of children who died within the Inn. But you and I both know about making assumptions, especially with ghosts.

Even though Room Number 6 is popular with those wanting to have a paranormal experience, people have been known to vacate the room in a state of panic before the night they paid for is over.

ROOM 932
THE ROOM WITH A BOO

Hotel Bethlehem
437 Main Street
Bethlehem, PA 18018

Some places tend to downplay it when some of their guests who have left their mortal existence behind stay on at the hostelry for one reason or another. You won't find this reticence at the Historic Hotel Bethlehem where the ghosts are welcomed and embraced.

The Hotel's website touts the fact that they

have no less than four spirits there who enjoy the facilities so much that they have taken up a kind of afterlife residence there.

One is a world-famous singer from the mid-nineteenth century who fell afoul of the Hope Diamond curse who hangs out at the 3rd floor exercise room and lobby areas.

Another is the bare-footed 1833 landlord of the hotel who was fired from her position along with her partner landlord and husband because of his penchant for spirituous drinks. She prefers the dining and food preparation areas.

Bethlehem's unofficial guide, known to one and all as Daddy Thomas passed away on April 4, 1822. But that hasn't caused him to stop dispensing good humor and advice from his digs within the boiler room of the hotel.

Finally we come to Room 932, known as the Room With a Boo. People have experienced apparitions and unexplainable activity in the room. One couple was confronted by a gentleman standing at the foot of their bed who inquired as to why they were in "his" room. When they turned on the bedside lamp, he disappeared. Lights turn on, and off, with no physical assistance and papers fly from the desk unaided by hand or breeze.

Then, there is the bathroom. Countless guests have seen someone other than themselves peering back at them from within the mirror. The fleeting apparition disappears as soon as they look over their shoulder to see who else my be in the room with them.

As near as can be determined, one of the spirits in the mirror is named Mary, but no other details have been determined about her.

Maybe, if you stay in that room, you might be able to get her to identify herself.

If you can't, don't fret. She is just one of many who have been seen in that mirror. You may encounter one of the others, who so far haven't ventured any names to investigators.

But get your reservations soon, because Room 932, the Room with a Boo, is the most popular room in this historic hotel.

THE HAUNTED HOUSE OF DUNMORE, PA

The real estate ad seemed innocuous enough.
It showed up in late 2013 as follows:

For Sale – 1901 Victorian Home
4 bedrooms
2-1/2 Baths
Hardwood Floors
Wet Bar
Desirable Neighborhood
$140, 000

Oh yeah, and it's, "Slightly haunted, nothing serious, though." Among the "slightly haunted" aspects of the home were phantom footsteps, strange knockings, and a "barely noticeable" scream usually at precisely 3:13AM, once a week.

Mentioned is also that "occasional ghastly visage lurking behind you in the bathroom mirror."

A firestorm of interest followed with the prospective sellers appearing on network TV shows and being featured in newspaper and magazine articles across the entire nation.

All this publicity bought about the desired results and the owners were inundated with inquiries, just none from actual serious prospective buyers. But every ghost hunter for miles around showed up, K-II meter and digital recorder in hand, to be given the grand tour. The owners should have been cautioned to "Be careful what you wish for – it just might be granted."

The home is no longer for sale, but has found a permanent listing in the annals of the Museum of Hoaxes, a self-described place where you can find, "Wonderful stories contrived for the public from ancient times to the present day." To find this museum, just drive northward on Interstate 5 from San Diego, California until you see the giant floating jackalope off to the right of the road.

Or you can check out the museum's website at hoaxes.org.

PART III

WINDOWS

WHY WINDOWS?

How do spirits get trapped in glass windows? I don't think they are *trapped* per se, so much as the windows *allow* them to manifest.

Window glass acts as a projection screen for spirits, especially in the area of residual hauntings. By flattening an amorphous misty apparition onto the glass, details that would be otherwise be lost become visible.

Spirits have no physical properties being composed entirely of energy or some other, unknown substantive material. Our complete non-physical being is stored within that wonderful computer known as our brain as electrical impulses, similar to the way information is stored on the hard drive of a computer.

Now, when our body, which serves as a container for our being, no longer exists, our psychical self lives on as those electrical impulses. But, the amount of energy that it has is only enough to allow it to cohere with none left over to allow it to manifest itself either visually or audibly. The spirit must absorb energy elsewhere in order to do this.

Heat is one of the sources of energy that spirits use to make themselves known, since heat is a form of energy. Other sources are batteries in portable devices, flowing water in rivers and streams, electrical supply lines, microwave transmitters, electrical storms, and snow storms.

Once the entity absorbs enough energy, it makes itself known in a variety of ways ranging from EVPs to orbs, mist, partial apparitions and full-body apparitions.

Often spirits appear as images in glass windows.

In the first report about spirits appearing in windows, Clyde Overholt at the Homestead House at West Overton Village, I will attempt to further explain this phenomenon.

CLYDE OVERHOLT

The Overholt Mansion
West Overton Village
Scottdale, PA

Nestled along a stream called variously Felgar Run or Joy Run that eventually trickles its way to the Youghiogheny River is a little settlement called West Overton Village, founded by Henry Overholt.

In April of 1800, Henry emigrated to this area just outside of what is now known as Scottdale, PA where he and his wife raised 12 children. There he founded a distillery where Old Overholt Rye

Whiskey was made, bottled, and shipped. It was a quite profitable endeavor and enabled him to build a substantive brick mansion adjacent to the distillery. The little village surrounding the distillery eventually grew to 19 buildings to support this enterprise.

Henry, and later his sons Abraham and Christian, ran the operation. Abraham bought out Christian and introduced the concept of vertical integration to the production of he whiskey. Vertical integration is a system whereby the producer of he final product owns and controls every aspect of the production of the final result, including all the ingredients. So, Abraham owned, not only the fields producing he rye for the whiskey, but also the distillery, the bottling plant, and the wagons used to deliver the whiskey.

His grandson, Henry Clay Frick, who was born on the premises, understood this concept and saw how it could be used in the production of other products to increase profitability. Henry Clay Frick used this process when making coke for the steel industry wherein he owned the mines, the coke ovens, the railroad sidings, and the railroad cars used to deliver it. When he met and partnered with Andrew Carnegie, he introduced vertical integration to the production of steel, eventually making both Andrew Carnegie and himself two of the richest men in the world.

The restored buildings, mansion, and distillery at West Overton Village is a tribute to the Overholt family and the birthplace of Henry Clay Frick.

The mansion, called the Homestead House is a three story brick edifice built in 1838 where various members and generations of the Overholt family lived until 1922 when it was sold to Helen Clay Frick, daughter of Henry Clay Frick.

Today, it is operated as a museum and tours of the buildings and grounds are conducted at various times.

As with any building that is rich in history and has existed for an extended period of time, the Homestead House has picked up its fair share of hauntings over the one and quarter plus centuries of its existence.

Many members of the Overholt family were born, lived, and died within the walls of the old mansion. Some of them left behind their earthly existence before their scheduled time to die.

One such was Clyde Overholt.

Clyde was born in 1876 into this great manufacturing family and, as such, enjoyed all the perks and benefits of a scion of wealth. In 1897, at the age of 21, Clyde was on the board of directors of the Scottdale Connecting Railroad, along with three other members of the close knit family. You might say he had money.

Clyde lived his entire life in the Homestead House with his doting mother, wanting for nothing. It must have been a devastating event in his life when, in 1921, his dear mother passed away.

During Clyde's life his brother, Christian, managed to also be on the board of directors of the Scottdale Connecting Railroad Company. However Christian also had a few enterprises of his own, moved out of the mansion at an early age, and started up his own companies.

There is no record of sibling rivalry between Clyde and Christian, but certain events suggest that it did exist. One on particular seems to have been the tipping point that sent Clyde over the edge.

Oral history reports that, while Clyde and family was attending the funeral of his mother, Christian has made arrangements to have most of the furniture and accouterments removed from the family mansion.

Clyde returned home from his mother's funeral to grieve in solitude, only to be confronted with an empty home, bereft of contents. This so affected him that he went to his bedroom on the upper floor, retrieved his shotgun from where he had left it in that room, placed the shotgun in his mouth, and pulled the trigger.

The *Scottdale Independent Observer* reported on his death and the finding of his body in its issue of November 17, 1921.

Starting shortly after Clyde's suicide, his visage has been seen looking pensively down from the window of his bedroom as though he was bidding farewell to the life he had known and that had been so nastily wrenched from his grasp at the death of his mother and the subsequent stripping of furnishings from the only home he had even known.

On one occasion I was inside the mansion when my friend, Nancy, called to me from outside. I went to the second floor porch at the rear of the mansion and asked her what she wanted. She said that she was observing Clyde looking from his window. I rushed back in the building, took the steps two at a time and dashed to Clyde's bedroom. Entering Clyde's bedroom I went to the window where Clyde was located.

I saw nothing inside the room. Neither mist, smoke, nor an apparition of any kind. I looked out the window and waved to my friend who was on ground level to the side of the house. She waved back and motioned me down. When I joined her in the side yard, she told me that she saw Clyde peering down on her until suddenly he disappeared and was replaced by me waving from the window.

This event was the one that convinced me that these manifestations of residual hauntings are contained solely within the window itself and not in the room where the window is located.

The best way I can define it is that it is like a hologram or remote projection that is somehow contained *within* the glass of the window and can only be seen from outside the building where the window is located.

If someone can give me an alternate definition or explanation that fits the criteria, I welcome it with both open arms and an open mind. I am not one of those paranormal investigators who considers himself an "expert." In this field there are no experts, only people who have found investigative techniques and theories that work for them. If you come across someone who says they have found the one and only answer, protect your wallet and run like the wind.

THE BABUSHKA LADY

Connellsville public library
299 South Pittsburgh Street
Connellsville, PA 15425

In spite of local opposition, the School Board, the Town Council, and the Library Committee decided in the late 1800s that the ideal place for the Carnegie Free Library of Connellsville would be where the old Connell Graveyard was located in the middle of town. The graveyard had to go and its occupants moved to Chestnut Hill Cemetery a quarter of a mile away. One of the occupants was

Zachariah Connell, the founder of both the town and the cemetery he had called home since 1813. Nobody consulted him for his opinion of the move.

* * *

The Connellsville Courier of April 20, 1900 describes this move under the headline,

"REMOVING THE DEAD From the Old Fourth Ward Graveyard Draws Morbid Crowds. "

"Morbid curiosity and the sympathy of friends and relatives for their dead is drawing many persons to the old grave yard in the Fourth Ward where Contractor Bernard O'Conner is removing the bodies from the site of the proposed free Carnegie library. Each headstone is numbered as it is removed and a small box is placed alongside of this headstone marked with the same number as the headstone. When the remains, what little of them is left, are uncovered they are carefully placed in the boxes and removed to the lot in Chestnut Hill Cemetery, where they are laid in their final resting places. Some of the friends of the long deceased complain of the removal of their dead, but in many instances they have given the graves so little attention that they cannot even locate them. In none of the graves so far opened is there but little trace of the body interred. Yesterday the body of

James Brierly, who was the first man killed on what is now the Pittsburg division of the Baltimore & Ohio railroad, was disinterred and there was considerable of the coffin intact. Brierly was killed at Shaner 41 years ago. The oldest gravestone standing in the cemetery bears the date of 1803, though there are said to be graves there dug well back in the seventies. In several instances two coffins have been found in the same grave one, being buried on top of the other. The headstone marked "1803" has a peculiar inscription on it resembling Indian signs and bears the initials "H. W."

* * *

In a matter of only a couple of years time, the new Carnegie Free Library of Connellsville swung its doors open in 1903 for the education and edification of the public. Shortly thereafter, specters made their presence known within its hallowed halls and stacks of books as ghostly footsteps resound when nobody is visible. Books fall from heir shelves unaided by any earthly presence.

A man and woman have been seen sitting quietly together within the library, only to disappear from sight when approached. If you stand outside the library, you may see an elderly woman wearing a babushka sitting inside one of the windows. Then, when you enter the library, not only isn't she at that window, nobody inside the library has seen her, or anyone else, at that window.

Why is this so? Nobody offers a definitive answer, but ever since the exhumation and removal of what was left of those who had been interred within the boundaries of the Old Connell Graveyard, rumors abounded that all the bodies hadn't been located and that some remain under the library building itself.

Nevertheless, they content themselves with minor distractions and appearances and don't even seem to be all that upset with heir lot. Maybe they enjoy the company of the library's patrons.

THE YOUNG LADY IN THE WINDOW

Kutztown Historical Society Building
Intersection of Normal Ave. and Whiteoak Street
Kutztown, PA

The Kutztown Historical Society was formed in 1975 just in time for the United States Bicentennial. Four years later, on February 27, 1979 it purchased the historic Kutztown Public School Building which was built in 1892. A point of interest is that this was he first public school building in Pennsylvania to have central heating. It was added to the National Registry of Historic Places in 1980. It now serves as the headquarters of the Kutztown Historical Society as well as a museum depicting the rich and varied history of the area.

The museum is chock full of artifacts including toys, tools, textile implements, fire and farm equipment, books, military and civilian equipment, all of cultural and historical significance to Kutztown and Berks County.

With the purchase of the building and the acquisition of countless items of historical significance, it is no small wonder that some of these things came with entities of otherworldly origination attached.

People have experienced being touched by unseen hands as they walk the hallways and spectral voices try to get attention, but they are coming from deserted areas.

One spirit in particular appears to be that of a young woman, whose origin is unknown. Speculation is that she may be the shade of a deceased student of the school or possibly even a long-gone teacher. Or, she may have even come to the building with one of the artifacts that are now on display there at the museum. Nobody knows for sure. But what is known for sure is that she has been seen by numerous people peering down on Normal Avenue looking or waiting for who knows what.

If you see her at one of those upper floor windows, don't look away. For as soon as you do, when you look back, she will be gone.

SAD LITTLE GIRL IN THE WINDOW

McCandless Township Town Hall
9955 Grubbs Rd.
Wexford, PA 15090

There is nothing special about the McCandless Township Town Hall. It's a relatively modern sprawling two-story brick and concrete building housing various offices and departments that run the township. Next door to the town hall is a larger variation of the Town Hall building that houses both the Public Works Department and the Police Department.

Both the Town Hall and the Public Works/Police Department buildings have been built on farm land, which is not unusual, since the entire area was farm land until the post World War Two population explosion gobbled up all available land in the suburbs and rural valleys north of Pittsburgh.

However, this particular plot of land was, and is, rumored to have been the location where a young child, supposedly a little girl, met her end in a particularly tragic manner. It was during the early 1900s when, while playing one day, she fell into a well. During the early twentieth century high-powered digging machines and well trained and equipped fire departments weren't readily available. As a result, she perished.

Police officers and dispatchers working the midnight shift report hearing phantom footsteps treading the stairs between the floors, disembodied voices whispering and mumbling indecipherable words, and doors creaking open and closed. Lights throughout the building have a penchant for turning on and off at random times when there is nobody in those areas. Plus, the building is locked during the overnight shift.

Others report seeing the appearance of a young child at one of the windows peering outward with a pensive, wistful expression as though she wished she could be out among the rolling grass-covered slopes and shade trees doing what young kids do best – playing.

Is it the shade of the youngster who lost her life in a well? Or is it someone else? Nobody seems to have a definitive answer. But everyone who has seen her remark on how sad she appears, seeming to be on the verge of tears. And, just as they wish they could just give her a hug to make her feel better, she disappears.

THE GRAY HAIRED LADY

The Whit-Mar Inn
Pottsville Pike
Reading, PA

Don't bother trying to find the Whit-Mar Inn at 3650 Pottsville Pike near Reading. It isn't there anymore. It was replaced years ago by, of all things, a Wa-Wa Convenience Store and Gas Station. No longer do locals belly up to the bar to partake of favorite libations. Meals today available at the Wa-Wa are definitely not of the home-cooked variety previously available at the former tavern and restaurant that was located on that spot.

And no longer can you see the spirit of an elderly lady looking out at you from one of the windows of the inn. She and her Native American companion, both of whom had been blamed for various otherworldly activity on the premises have gone the way of the inn's component structural parts, probably to a landfill. No longer will patrons and employees be treated to such things as doors randomly slamming shut and lights turning on and off without rhyme nor reason. The spirit of the old woman no longer alleviates the chills in her bones by shutting down the air conditioning of the inn.

Modernization and progress have evicted two colorful and beloved spirits from their haunt. Let's all say a prayer that they aren't just free-floating in some ethereal dimension, but have found peace in the hereafter.

THE HAND PRINT

Williamson College of the Trades
106 South New Middletown Road
Media, PA 19063

Founded in 1888 by Isiah Vansant Williamson as the Williamson Free School of Mechanical Trades, this educational institute has been providing the nation with well taught young men in the fields of building trades since its inception.

It sits on a wooded and grass-covered knoll alongside a tree-lined lane in Media, PA about a dozen miles west of the City of Philadelphia, creating an island of rural serenity in the bustling populated area, a stone's throw from US Route 1.

Today, the school, now named the Williamson College of the Trades graduates students with Associates Degrees in any of the trades offered, including Carpentry, Machine Tool Technology, Power Plant Technology, Horticulture, Masonry, Landscaping, or Painting. What really sets this school apart is that no student who attends has ever had to pay for tuition or room and board. Both the school's founder Isiah Williamson and a major endowment from the John Wannamaker Foundation has seen to that.

As with any institution that has over a century of history attached to it, the college has also picked up a few haunts through the years. George Dormitory, a student housing unit that was once used as a recovery unit for returning soldiers who were graduates of the school, echoes late at night with phantom footsteps and people who visit there during those hours come away with an uncomfortable feeling of having been watched.

At Rowan Hall, previously just called The Main Building, where school founder Williamson is supposed to have been buried under the steps, people report a sensation of "strange feelings" when standing there at night. Supposedly your body will cast shadows in four directions simultaneously while standing there and Old Isiah Willamson's ghost has been observed in the same vicinity.

Finally, over at Longstreth Dormitory a window seems to be haunted by a reappearing hand print. No matter how many times the window is washed and made to sparkle in the sunlight, within a day or two, the hand print comes back as though it had never been wiped away.

FACE IN THE WINDOW

The Old Village Inn
Intersection of Route 23 and Mill Road
Morgantown, PA

Back in 1770, Captain Jacob Morgan, a veteran of the French and Indian War, laid out the town aptly named after himself. This was shortly after he built a large stone house on Hartz Road which is one of many homes rumored to have been a place where George Washington spent a restful night during his military career.

Today, Morgantown lies near the intersection of Routes I-76, I-175, and PA 23 making it both a transportation hub and an ideal location for manufacturing and distribution in the Reading/ Philadelphia corridor.

Right in the middle of Morgantown on PA Route 23 at Mill Road is the Old Village Inn, built in the late 1800s. It was once a combination hotel, restaurant and bar that served both the people of the town and anyone passing through who needed a place to stay. In its heyday, the Inn was a favored place to stay for wealthy travelers from Philadelphia who were en route to western destinations. However, since the growth of the town and the arrival of large chain motels, the Inn no longer provides overnight accommodations and operates as a local tavern and restaurant providing food and entertainment for its clientele.

But this is not to say that the rooms once occupied by people escaping the heat and dust of the big city are empty. Oh no - a couple of former patrons of the Inn, a man and woman dressed in what appears to be early twentieth century garb walk the halls of the second floor where the guest rooms were once located.

And, should you stand across Route 23, also called Main Street, and look at the Inn, you may be one of those who see an indistinct face looking back from one of the second floor widows. Don't even bother to go into the bar or the restaurant to inquire about it. The staff will assure you there is nobody up there and that the rooms facing the street are empty. Nobody knows whose face appears in the window and likewise, nobody know where it came from.

THE CHILDREN OF THE

Clay Street School
Kane, PA

The elementary school sits a bit back from the sidewalk on Clay Street in Kane, PA behind a weed-choked fence. Looking at it through the tall iron gate, the building looms balefully even in the bright sunlight of a summer day.

Time was when the place was overgrown with children laughing and playing rather than unmowed weeds. The windows sparkled in the daylight and bright lights shone through the windows on overcast days while the kids were studying their three Rs.

The Clay Street School was one of those anomalies where the neighborhood children actually walked to school instead of being delivered there by a big yellow behemoth.

Those children have long ago grown into adults and the school just sits on its one acre lot mourning their absence.

However, after the sun slips below the western horizon and darkness engulfs the area, passersby have reported seeing the faces of children looking down on them from the second story windows. Maybe the building itself is reliving better days. The observation is made most frequently at roughly 2 AM.

I was unable to see the little urchins peering down from their high windows, but I was only there twice and probably missed a time when they had accumulated enough energy to make an appearance.

PART IV

PHANTOM MUSIC

WHAT IS PHANTOM MUSIC?

People have *seen* apparitions. They have *felt* spirits making themselves known by extracting energy in the form of heat from the environment causing "cold spots." Frequently we have *smelled* aromas of pipe tobacco, perfumes, and other smells where they shouldn't exist. These are some of the ways we use our senses to notice entities who call the after-world home.

Hearing is one of our five, some people say six, senses. And it is no surprise that spirits reveal themselves to us auditorily as well. You're probably familiar with EVPs, Electronic Voice Phenomena, whereby denizens of the spiritual plane make themselves known by imprinting their voice electronically on digital recorders by utilizing the energy contained within the devices' batteries.

Phantom Music is something altogether different. It occurs when a denizen of the afterlife haunts a musical instrument in such a way as to produce actual music from the instrument. These musical strains are surprisingly heard by witnesses with no electronic go-between needed to record the recital.

Interesting enough, the musical instruments involved almost always involve a keyboard instrument such as a piano, organ, or harpsichord.

Although I have investigated at least one instance of phantom bagpipe music and have had reported to me events including fifes and drums and bugle calls at various battlefield.

The following examples are items that have musically-inclined spirits attached to them in such a way that they create music for us to hear.

Kinda reminds me of a song my mom used to sing while she was doing various chores around the house when I was a just a tyke.

She would happily warble, "I hear music and there's no one there. I smell blossoms and the trees are bare. All night long I'm walking on air. I wonder why. I wonder why."

Who woulda thunk that, all these years later, that song would come back to haunt me?

Anyhow, here's a couple of examples ...

THE SPECTRAL PIANO

Central Catholic High School
1400 Hill Road
Reading, PA

In 1939, Reverend William Hammeke, rector of St. Paul's Church in Reading, purchased the Bon Air mansion built by William Luden of Luden's

Cough Drop fame for the local Catholic Diocese. The intention was to turn it into a Catholic High School, which was done. The building's highlight and crowning jewel was the beautiful marble staircase that wound up to the second floor.

The school opened its door to students in 1940 with an inaugural class of 75 students. The enrollment never exceeded 300 during its 61 years of existence.

According to locals, the son of Mr. Luden, William Junior, called Billy, committed suicide on the third floor of the mansion by hanging himself. Other accounts say that he did it on the elevated porch that wraps around a goodly part of the building's second floor. All accounts agree that his spirit still inhabits the building, along with a number of other spectres. They all join together, making themselves known in a variety of ways.

Teachers and students alike have had the experience of seeing lights turn on and off with no earthly input. Extreme cold spots were encountered in many of the rooms and custodians reported hearing doors opening and slamming shut accompanied by phantom footsteps when they knew they were the only ones in the building. The apparition of a young man thought to be Billy has been seen standing on the front portico and that of an older woman glides regally down the aforementioned marble staircase.

Perhaps most strangely of all is the piano. When the mansion was purchased by the Allentown Diocese, some things came with it. One of those was Mr. Luden's piano in the drawing room. It is unknown whether Mr. Luden played it himself or merely enjoyed hearing someone else do so. It has even been speculated that young Billy took lessons on it.

Nevertheless, the piano has been heard many times emitting music when there was no one even in the room with it to play it. Some thought it was young Billy tickling the ivories as a playful prank. But that's not all. Mr. Luden's piano was eventually removed from the premises and sold, donated, or otherwise disposed elsewhere. Most of us would think that would solve the problem of phantom music. But such was not to be the case. The inexplicable resonance of piano music has continued to be heard echoing in the halls of the building even to this day. So, not only is the pianist a spectral one, the piano itself is a ghostly instrument as well.

Then, due to financial constraints, Reading Central Catholic High School merged with Holy Name High School and became Berks Catholic High School at Holy Name's location on East Wyomissing Blvd.

As of this writing, the Bon Air Mansion is lying fallow and tenant-less. But, plans are in motion for it to be the location of the new Berks Charter High School for the Performing and Visual Arts hopefully to open in 2021 after the Covid 19 Virus is defeated. Then, when these new students are practicing lines and choreography for the stage, maybe, just maybe, they will hear piano accompaniment, courtesy of the phantom musician playing on his invisible piano.

THE HAUNTED RADIO

Days Inn(Now Closed)
18360 Conneaut Lake Road
Meadville, PA

The former Days Inn in Meadville was rife with hauntings from apparitions to non-corporeal entities following you in the hallway. Those stalkers could only be seen as reflections in the window at the end of that hallway. Other spirits in the smaller, detached building caused weird sounds throughout and turned lights on and off at random times.

In the kitchen area was a radio that insisted on playing its choice of music whether or not anyone else wanted to hear it. One evening in particular, the night shift security guard was making his rounds when he heard music being played in the deserted kitchen. He entered the area and traced the sounds to a radio sitting on a counter. It was tuned to a local music station. No problem – he simply turned the radio off and started walking away. Imagine his surprise when the radio came back on playing music again before he even left the kitchen. So he walked back to the radio and turned it off again, this time making sure that it was actually off. Then he left continuing on his rounds.

A while later, as he traversed the hallway outside the kitchen, he heard the strains of music coming from the kitchen yet one more time. This time, he went to the radio and verified that it was actually turned off while it was playing. So, he unplugged it and wasn't bothered by the radio's choice of music any more that night. But, kitchen workers have said that it happened so often while they were in the kitchen that they just ignored it and allowed the spirit to listen to whatever music the he or she enjoyed. Maybe it was listening to one of those stations that play, "The music of your afterlife."

Now, the Days Inn is gone. It closed once and for all and, as of 2017, the property was purchased by a non-profit group who will remodel it, then reopen it as a senior-housing facility. While some of the other otherworldly occupants may remain, the radio is now long-gone. I wonder if it was taken by a former employee of the Inn, thrown away, or sold at auction with the rest of the furnishings. In any case, it is probably still playing the music the haunt who is attached to it prefers to listen to, whether it is on or off, plugged in or not.

THE PIANO
OF OLD STATE ROAD

Pine Grove, PA

As you approach the little town of Pine Grove, PA, a few miles east and north of Harrisburg, a small two-lane road parallels Interstate 81. It has a bit of an identity problem, going by both the name of Old State Road and Bear Hole Trail. The so-called "road" is nothing more than a semi-graded gravel path with vehicular traffic banned from it for years since it's designation as a hiking trail through the little known Swatara State Park. So, perhaps the moniker Bear Hole Trail is a more appropriate appellation.

Years ago there was a stately old frame home along the road. A totally unverifiable rumor about the home said that an elderly man was hanged within the house by construction workers who were there to renovate the building. No mention was ever made concerning what the gent did to incite the workers to this murderous level of retribution. However, mention *was* made that the rope used to hang him was still dangling in the attic. Probably a case of trespassers in an abandoned house finding the rope in the attic and fabricating a story to go with it.

93

There is yet another story about the house. It was bandied about that the house had an old upright piano in one of the rooms. The piano was in a state of disrepair, a number of keys missing, and some of the wooden frame broken. But that didn't prevent spectral hands from tickling the ivories and causing gossamer tunes to waft on the midnight air.

All things come to an end and this is no exception. The building was demolished in June of 2008 meaning that neither event can be investigated, much less verified.

This one doesn't even rise to the level of myth, let alone folk lore.

But, should you find yourself leisurely strolling along this gently winding trail on some summer evening at sunset, cock your ears and listen intently. If you hear the off-key tinkling of a honky-tonk tune melodiously wending its way through the forest, drop me a line. I love being proved wrong.

ELEVEN HAUNTED PIANOS

Saint Mary's Hall
Villanova University
800 Lancaster Ave
Villanova, PA

Villanova University is rife with hauntings of all kinds and Saint Mary's Hall is the epicenter of the paranormal activity at this institute of higher learning.

Saint Mary's Hall is one of the oldest buildings on the campus, having been originally used as a seminary. Today, it houses a bit over 200 students. It is wonderfully self-contained, having a dining hall, a convenience store, gym, locker room and even a swimming pool. There are also administration offices on site and it is the location of the university's Music Activity Program.

As part of the Music Program, the building has an area called St. Mary's Chapel which is actually the auditorium, home to the Student Theater Group, the Villanova Singers, the university's Jazz Festival and a host of other performers and events.

The "Chapel" is equipped with all the various and sundry things that you would expect of an area used as an entertainment venue: stage, seating, sound system, and so on. In addition, probably from its days as a chapel, it has a functional organ to provide music to accompany the stage productions.

One day in 2009, Senior Resident Assistant Marissa Crispa was strolling through the building when she happened on a group of students clustered around the door leading into the chapel.

With her interest piqued, she investigated and joined them. As she approached the door, she heard the definite tones of organ music originating from within the chapel and floating on the air to be heard outside the partially opened doors.

One of the young ladies in the group at the door motioned Marissa over and pointed into the chapel, specifically where the organ was located. Marissa looked in that direction and saw the organ bathed in a puddle of yellow light from the lamp that sat upon it to allow the organist to read the music he or she was playing.

Up to this point nothing was out of the ordinary. That is until Marissa noticed that there was no organist at the instrument. Phantom hands were plying the keys and phantom feet were treading the pedals!

And this was neither the first nor the last time that the phantom organist of St. Mary's Chapel gave a recital. However it was one of the few times that more than just a couple of people heard the otherworldly strains of etudes in a minor key drifting in the wee hours of the night.

At other times the phantom tickles the ivories on one of the eleven pianos situated throughout the building ranging from modern uprights to a baby grand. It is often assumed that the tinkling of piano music being heard in the building is the work of one of the music students practicing his or her art. But, too many times to count, a security person has traveled in the direction of the music because it is being played after reasonable hours and may distract others from their rest or studying. The security guard tracks the music to one of the classrooms from which the music is emanating only to find the room locked. He fumbles for his key, unlocks and opens the door to remonstrate with the erstwhile musician only to witness the music falling silent and, not only is there nobody seated at the piano, there is no corporeal body within the room ... other than the security guard.

And there are other spirits residing within St. Mary's Hall to distract students and faculty alike giving it the reputation of being the most haunted building on campus.

There is a phantom music-loving aficionado in the premises who, like the spirit at the old Days Inn in Meadville, described elsewhere in this book, enjoys listening to the radio during the wee hours of the morning. From time-to-time janitorial employees have said that they have walked by a room that has a radio within blasting music at full volume. Then, when they enter the room, they find it to be empty of living human occupants. And the music immediately stops as they enter. When the radio is checked, it is found to be unplugged!

Elsewhere in the building is a music room equipped with a piano. Security guards making their late night rounds have heard strains of piano music being played. But when they enter the room to check it out, they find that they are the only one in the room.

And lest somebody want to blame this activity on collegiate pranksters, the occurrences seem to happen most frequently between sessions when students are off-campus and the dorms are unoccupied.

THE HAUNTED ORGAN

Seton Hill University
Greensburg

In 1918, as World War I came to an end, the Catholic Sisters of Charity opened a small liberal arts college for women in Greensburg. Since that time it has grown into a moderate-size coeducational university with several thousand

100

students, and the buildings and grounds have become populated with their share of ghostly presences.

In the Administration building, which was once the mother house, people hear the pounding of fists on wood late at night. A rather apocryphal tale has it that, in the early twentieth century, an elderly nun fell asleep in the basement. Supposedly a custodian saw her lying there and assumed that she was dead. She was buried alive. She awakened in her coffin and beat on the lid until she died for real. It is her spirit pounding in the late hours in the Administration Building.

I have been told that I am an unusually sound sleeper, having slept through the sounds of thunderstorms, passing railroad trains, and even a vehicle accident outside my bedroom window. But even if this elderly nun was twice as sound a sleeper as I am, she probably would have awakened when the undertaker inserted a large needle into her femoral artery to replace her blood with embalming fluid.

The late-night sounds at the Administration Building may be of otherworldly origin, but they are probably not generated by a prematurely buried nun.

The spirits of teaching nuns long deceased walk from one classroom to another in the labyrinthine corridors of Maura Hall. If you meet up with one of them, don't bother to ask for directions. She won't answer you.

Brownlee Residence is a dorm for freshman women, and some of the young ladies report that their sleep is disturbed at night by someone running up and down the hallway on the first floor. When a resident opens her door to investigate or remonstrate, no one is ever there, even as the sounds continue. One of the first-floor dorm rooms has a mysterious purple light in the corner of the room. The shadow of a girl who hanged herself many years ago is said to be imprinted on the hall wall across from the room where she ended her life. A ghost of a priest hurries across the main parking lot heading in the general direction of the Administration Building. Possibly he is heading for St. Joseph's Chapel, late for vespers.

Speaking of St. Joseph's Chapel, a ghostly nun has been seen in the room directly to the right of the organ. The organ door opens and closes, seemingly on its own, and ghostly hymns waft in the still air of the chapel as an unseen chorus sings.

On foggy evenings and the predawn hours, a woman stops traffic on the main driveway. When a driver stops the car for her, she fades into the fog.

A little boy plays with a ball nearby on the

grass. When disturbed he gathers up his ball and runs into oblivion, screaming all the while as though being chased.

Indistinct shapes wander the sisters' cemetery, hovering over the graves.

THE SELF-PLAYING PLAYER PIANO

Historic Hotel Bethlehem
437 Main Street
Bethlehem

Across the street from the Moravian Book Shop sits the majestic Hotel Bethlehem. Its spectral residents aren't quite as helpful as the one at the bookstore, but they are quite entertaining nevertheless.

In 1741, Moravian missionaries built on the site of today's hotel the "First House of Bethlehem." At the time, that solitary building sat on the bank of a fresh running stream in the middle of the wilderness. On December 24 of that year, Christmas Eve, Count Nicholas Von Zinzendorf, a Moravian patron traveling under the name of Domine de Thuirstein, sang a hymn about Bethlehem, and the decision was made to name the little settlement after the location of Christ's birth.

In 1794, the Golden Eagle Hotel was erected on that spot. It served tourists and business travelers for the next century and a quarter before coming to the end of its days as a convalescent home for wounded soldiers returning home from World War I. The Golden Eagle Hotel closed its doors in April of 1919.

Three years later, after an infusion of $800,000 from steel magnate Charles M. Schwab and other Bethlehem businessmen, the world-class historic Bethlehem Hotel opened its doors. It immediately became *the* place to stay in eastern Pennsylvania. It was host to five Presidents of the United States, Winston Churchill, the Prime Minister of Great Britain, the Dalai Lama, and countless A-list entertainers and sports figures.

During Prohibition, the hotel boasted a hidden speakeasy. For a while, it sold its own brand of cigars. The tile on the floor in the fabulous 1741 on the Terrace Dining Room was made at the Moravian Tile Works in Doylestown. It is the same Moravian tile found in Pennsylvania's Capitol building in Harrisburg, as well as in the world-famous Monte Carlo Casino in Monte Carlo.

The hotel changed hands after 1960 and fell on hard times for a short while before being brought back to its original splendor and elegance by Robert and Dee Decker, Bethlehem developers who purchased it in 1984.

With all this history it would be unconscionable for the stately building to be without ghosts. Not to disappoint anyone, it is filled to the rafters with spirits of all types, mostly benign. It is commonplace for both visitors and staff to encounter shadows that fade as quickly as they appear, see transparent figures roaming the halls and stairwells, or hear the elevator operated by an unseen being. The cold spots cannot be attributed to anomalies in the state-of-the-art heating system, and you just may feel a tap on the shoulder or hear your name called when you think you are alone.

And that's just the anonymous spirits roaming about. A raft of colorful people who enjoyed their stays at the hotel so much that their spirits decided to stay on are well known.

One has been identified as Francis "Daddy" Thomas, a devout Moravian who was famous for his fearlessness in the face of danger. In his younger days, around the 1750s, he was a courier, delivering mail and dispatches through the Indian-controlled area. At that time, couriers faced several dangers – not only roaming Indian bands but also marauding thieves, since they were often known to carry valuables. Once Daddy was thrown from his horse so severely that he fractured his neck and was carried home on a litter, assumed to be dead. But he escaped the Reaper that time and recovered. Another time he plunged through thick ice on horseback into frigid waters, exposing himself to the dual dangers of drowning and exposure. Once again, he cheated Death and recovered.

Daddy Thomas eventually gave up his life of danger and became a cabinetmaker, married, and settled down. Although he and his wife had no children of their own during their 53-year marriage, they raised three children of Moravian missionaries. All three were sent to study at the famous Moravian Girls' Seminary at Bethlehem.

During all those years, Daddy was Bethlehem unofficial ambassador, welcoming everyone who visited the town. He became famous for his kindness and upbeat disposition and was a favorite of townspeople and travelers as well.

After his death in 1822, Daddy Thomas stayed

on to watch over and welcome people to the place he loved so much when he was alive.

Wearing his black tricorn hat and a long, black woolen cape, he has been spotted in the boiler room of the hotel near a filled-in escape tunnel used by the Moravians to avoid capture during Indian raids. He once appeared to a night engineer before disappearing in a puff of smoke that traveled across the boiler room. That engineer took to locking himself in his office and observed shadows moving on the floor through the space at the bottom of the locked door. He need not have worried about any harmful intentions on the part of Daddy Thomas, who just seems to be concerned with the welfare of guests, especially female, who check in at the hotel.

Two other colorful ghosts are a married couple, the Brongs. In 1833, after serving as managers of the hotel for a short six months, they were asked to leave by a committee of the Moravian Church, owner of the hotel at that time. The churchmen were less than appreciative of the Brongs' intemperate habits.

Mr. Brong had the habit of joining nearly every hotel guest to help them slake their thirst and wash the dust from their throats. So much so that the bartender routinely had to just about carry Mr. Brong to a nearby bench when he could no longer stand unassisted.

While Mr. Brong was offending hotel guests with his frequent intoxication, Mrs. Brong was equally offensive to early 19th-century sensibilities in her own way. She had the scandalous habit of walking about barefoot – as one guest put it, with her "pedal extremities completely exposed."

The Brongs left the hotel at the request of the church committeemen, but Mrs. Brong wasn't that easy to get quit of. Although the exact date of her demise isn't a matter of record, she came back to spend her afterlife at the hotel where she was once asked to leave.

Mrs. Brong is often seen in the kitchen and dining areas of the Hotel Bethlehem, wearing clothing appropriate to her era, with one exception that pretty much identifies her: the apparition lacks both shoes and stockings. You might say that her pedal extremities are completely exposed.

Mary Augusta Yohe, called "May" by one and all, was born at the Eagle Hotel in April 1866. Her grandfather, Caleb Yohe, was then the popular innkeeper. May was blessed with a beautiful voice and a talent for dancing. She often entertained hotel guests in the lobby. Her talent was so obvious and beguiling that the Moravians took up a collection and sent her to Paris for formal operatic training.

Twenty years later she was recognized as one

of the country's biggest stars, and her personal appearances always caused a sensation. She was the headliner wherever she went. Unfortunately, her rapid rise to stardom had an effect that we often seen today on young people thrust into celebrity before they achieve personal maturity. Her fame deteriorated into notoriety as her many flings became gossip fodder for the masses.

During the 1890s, May went to England for a command performance for Queen Victoria's son, Prince Edward, who adored her beautiful singing. While there, she met Lord Francis Clinton Hope, who owned the famous Hope diamond. She married him in short order. May was known to wear the diamond on certain occasions, despite the famous curse on it. Since its supposed theft from the forehead of an Indian idol in 1642, bad luck and death have been levied upon all who own or even touch it.

Whether the curse is true or not, Lord Hope was forced to sell the diamond in 1899 due to impending bankruptcy. May left him for the arms of a handsome American soldier the following year. May's choice was an unfortunate one, as the soldier stole all her jewelry and left her in the lurch. They reconciled, but then they broke up again, divorcing in 1905.

May's escapades damaged her popularity. She tried many comebacks, with limited success. Along with her third husband, John Smuts, she descended into poverty. She took on jobs as a janitor, a scrub woman, and a housekeeper. At the time of her death at the age of 72 in 1938, she was working as a clerk for the Works Progress Administration (WPA) earning $16.50 per week.

More than 3,000 people attended May's funeral that August and her husband, following her wishes, scattered her ashes in the Atlantic Ocean.

Since that time, May has returned to the place where she found the most happiness, the Bethlehem Hotel. To this day she gives impromptu performances in the lobby. The antique player piano located there is known to start up on its own, playing out favorites of yesteryear. Many people think she has something to do with that. Furthermore, she has made appearances on the third floor in the exercise room. And the smiling little girl who is seen beaming from random hotel windows sure resembles her description at an early age. [Could add some thoughts on whether ghosts can come back at different ages rather than just their age at death.]

Finally, there is Room 932, the Hotel Bethlehem's "room with a boo." People who have lodged overnight in that room have encountered many strange things. One couple was confronted by a man standing at the foot of their bed asking, "Why are you in my room?" When they turned on the light, he disappeared. Others have witnessed papers standing upright on the desk with no hands to hold them. Papers have also flown off the desk with no hands to throw them. Lamps in the room flash on, then off. At least one witness saw the wallpaper in the bathroom was turn pink, and numerous "orbs" have appeared in pictures taken in Room 932.

A paranormal investigator who overnighted in Room 932 came away with an armful of EVPs. Some of the statements recorded from unseen speakers:

"I've locked myself in the closet."

"Look out the window."

"What a beautiful bathroom."

"It's Mary."

If you want to stay in Room 932, you'd better book far in advance. It is probably the most popular room in the hotel.

THE PIPING HIGHLANDER

Macy's Department Store
400 Fifth Avenue
Pittsburgh

In 1871, the Kaufmannn brothers, Isaac and Jacob, opened a relatively small men's clothing store on the South Side of Pittsburgh. Six years later, they moved to this central location in downtown Pittsburgh. Known as the Big Store, it was owned and operated for most of the 20th century by Edgar J. Kaufmann. You may have heard of one of Mr. Kaufmann's other properties,

Fallingwater. It was designed by world-famous architect Frank Lloyd Wright and is located some 50 miles south of Pittsburgh in Mill Run, PA.

Kaufmann's was Pittsburgh's most successful department store. It watched all of its competitors fall by the wayside and has been operating under the Macy's name since 2005. But to this day, Pittsburghers still call it Kaufmann's.

And now, even Macy's has, so to speak, "Left the building,"falling prey to the ever-changing financial vagaries of the consuming public.

The building housing the store was built on the ground where Grant's Hill once was located. Grant's Hill was named after British Major James Grant, who was defeated by a coalition of French colonists and indigenous Indians from Fort Duquesne on September 14, 1758. As Downtown expanded, more and more of Grant's Hill was cut away to be used for building.

The tenth floor of the building was the ground level at the time of the battle. One of Major Grant's Highlanders who was killed during the battle haunts that tenth floor. Night cleaning staffers often hear his footsteps marching back and forth on the tiled floor while ghostly bag piping floats on the still air.

I have tried but had been unable to hear anything on that floor during store hours. The din

114

of shoppers, background music, and cash registers overcame anything ethereal.

And now, the lone piper is forced to tread the deserted floor waiting for new development to take place in the empty building. Perhaps at some future time when the edifice is re-purposed into upscale apartments for city dwellers, they will hear the strains of bagpipe music filtering through along the hallways of the venerable building.

THE ETHEREAL PIANIST

Mansfield University's
North Hall
31 South Academy Street
Mansfield, PA 16933

Mansfield University opened in 1857 as Mansfield Classical Seminary which later became Mansfield Normal School, then Mansfield State Teacher's College, then Mansfield State College, and finally in 1963, the Mansfield University.

One item of note is that the first night collegiate football game in the United States was played there in 1892 when Mansfield Normal and Wyoming Seminary played to a draw.

North Hall at Mansfield University is an imposing rectangular building taking up the space of two football fields and raising more than six stories high. Among other things, such as a cafeteria that comfortably seated 500 students, it served as housing for female classmates.

It's main interior feature is an atrium that extends from the ground floor six stories up to where the female dormitories were located.

During the period between 1908 and 1930, a young lady by name of Sara is aid to have fallen

116

over the railing of the uppermost floor resulting in her death. In any case, her body was found crumpled on the ground floor six floors below. Some people have said that she intentionally jumped to her death. The reason that it had to have happened between 1908 and 1030 is that the atrium was boarded up in 1930 for fear that it was a fire hazard.

For years afterward, the imprint of her body could be observed from time-to-time on that floor and diaphanous piano music attributed to her was heard wafting down from the sixth floor. But, no matter how quickly people rushed to investigate, the source of the music could never be found.

PART V

OTHER OBJECTS
OTHER HAUNTED ITEMS

Of course there are many, many other items that have gathered the interest of spirits besides mirrors, windows, keyboards, and rocking items. The rest of this book is dedicated to these.

Read on and enjoy ...

THE CHAIR OF DEATH

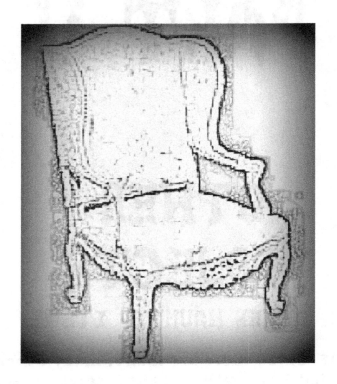

Baleroy Mansion
111 West Mermaid Lane
Chestnut Hill
Philadelphia

Of course a 32 room mansion built in 1911 on the whimsically named Mermaid Lane would have to have something associated with it to equal the fanciful title of its location. And so it is. Baleroy Mansion is one of many places that share the title of, "Most Haunted Home in America." Whether it is or not is open to conjecture, but it can at least lay claim to being the most haunted home in Philadelphia.

Its builder and first owner has been reported to have been a carpenter who probably lived in the carriage house, not the main mansion. He supposedly murdered his wife somewhere on the premises of the main house thus starting a long line of possible phantasms who call the place home.

A dozen or so years later, in 1926 the property was purchased by the Easby family who trace their lineage back to Easby Abbey in 12th Century England, Members of this family traveled to the New World with William Penn aboard the *HMS Welcome* and include at least three signers of the United States Declaration of Independence. The estate was furnished with items that traced their ownership to various notables including Napoleon, Thomas Jefferson, and General George Meade of Civil War fame.

It was given the name Baleroy by George Meade Easby, the great grandson of General Meade after Cheateau de Balleroy in the Normandy area of France. I guess you could say that this aristocratic family was living in the manner to which we would dearly like to become accustomed. It's the afterlife that goes on here that I wouldn't necessarily want to join.

Paranormal events in this mansion started shortly after the Easby family took possession and included George Meade Easby's brother Steven's reflection transforming into a flesh-less grinning skull before his very eyes. Perhaps this mirror was simply giving him a portent of things to come. That's because he died shortly thereafter of a childhood disease. Steven's ghost has been seen all around the mansion ever since in many forms. He is joined by his mother, Thomas Jefferson, an unknown elderly lady, and some prankster ghosts who play with the building's alarm system. They have done this so often that, according to "Haunted Houses, USA," written by Delores Riccio and John Bingham and published in 1989 that the local police who respond to those alarms now list "ghosts" in their reports as the cause of the alarm. All this is accompanied by the usual, for this place, random knocks, foot steps, and moving objects.

And speaking of objects, the most haunted object in the mansion, or should we say "cursed" is a 200-year-old wing back chair that was once owned by Napoleon. It innocently sits in a drawing room known as the Blue Room within the main house, quietly awaiting its next victim.

George Easby himself warned visitors and family alike not to sit in that chair that he dubbed, "The Death Chair," going to far as to drape a rope across it from arm to arm as a safeguard. To partake of its comfy cushions, was, according to George, tantamount to attempting to defy death, something that cannot be done. He felt that the chair was haunted by the malevolent spirit of a ghost named Amanda. Amanda is a wicked entity roaming the mansion who rips doors open and slams them shut with great ferocity. She has never been seen as a partial or full body apparition, only as a cold red mist hanging in the area between the Main Reception Room and the Blue Room where she attempts to entice the unwary into sitting in the Death Chair.

So far, at least three people have fallen under her spell and taken up her invitation to sit in that chair which folklore says was constructed in the 18th century by an evil warlock. George Meade Easby said that his housekeeper, his cousin, and a friend all went to their final resting place within weeks of taking what they thought was a temporary respite in the clutches of the chair.

Haunted, cursed, or folklore? And George is no longer available for interviews, having gone on to his own final rest on December 11, 2005. The current owners are using it as a private residence and no longer allow any tours or paranormal investigations to take place there.

A HAUNTED FIREPLACE

Fort Mifflin
1 Fort Mifflin Rd.
Philadelphia, PA 19153

A Short History

Fort Mifflin, originally called Fort Island Battery and Mud Island Fort was commissioned along the western bank of the Delaware River in 1771 to protect the colonial port of Philadelphia,

124

then the richest British port in the New World. Squabbling over its expense prevented it from being useful for its intended purpose until its completion in 1776. In 1795, the fort was officially named after Thomas Mifflin, a Continental Army officer who became the first Governor of the Commonwealth of Pennsylvania in the newly-formed United States of America.

The original fort was in continuous use until 1954 when it was decommissioned. In 1962 it was deeded over to the City of Philadelphia and, in 1970 was named a National Historic Landmark.

One of its nicknames is "The Fort That Saved America" because of the way the small garrison of 400 men kept the entire British Navy bottled up in the Delaware River during the fall of 1777. For six weeks, the fort kept up cannon fire preventing the British ships from proceeding up the Delaware to resupply the captured city of Philadelphia, all the while being incessantly bombarded by those same ships. During the hours of darkness, the garrison would be directed by French Major Francois de Fleury in repairing the damage done during the day. Finally, on November 15, 1777, with British ships pounding the fort from both upstream and downstream, the fort was evacuated and set ablaze by the last defenders to leave. At one point during the final days of the fort, over 1,000 cannon shells per hour rained down on its defenders.

From the original 400 man garrison at the fort, only 150 survived the battle unscathed. This six-week battle that hindered the British in their attempt to resupply their garrisons in occupied Philadelphia allowed General George Washington and the ravaged Continental Army the time to retreat to Valley Forge where they would spend winter and reorganize in order to go on to eventually defeat the British.

Fort Mifflin itself is still within the boundaries of the US. Army Corps of Engineers base at Hog Island and it is the only American Fort that actually predates the founding of the country.

During the Civil War, it was used as a POW camp and prison for captured Confederate soldiers. At the same time, it was used as a prison for Union soldiers convicted of various crimes and was the scene of numerous escape attempts. Although there were only 4 executions performed at the fort, several more prisoners died there due to untreated wounds and sickness brought on by the unsanitary conditions.

During World Wars I and II the fort was the site of an extensive ammunition storage depot, so much so that some citizens of the nearby city became nervous.

Fort Mifflin and Paranormal Activity

Because of its rich and intense history, Fort Mifflin has come to be regarded as on of the most haunted sites in the country. Some of the spirits encountered within its walls include the shade of Elizabeth Pratt, who hanged herself within the confines of the fort's Officers' Quarters and is often referred to by those who meet her as "the screaming woman.

A former executive director of the historic fort encountered a Civil War officer who felt that the stairway to the second story was unsafe and tried to prevent her from going to the second floor.

Another instance in the Officers' Quarters found a tour guide being awakened by a sharp knocking on the door to his room precisely at 3AM every time he would sleep over in that location. 3AM was the time military men would be awakened so that they could take over the next watch at the fort. This duty was preformed by the Messenger of the Watch whose spirit possibly mistook the sleeping tour guide for a soldier scheduled for the next watch.

Next to the Officers' Quarters is the Soldiers' Quarters where the Lamplighter still makes his rounds lighting the unseen oil lamps of a long gone era.

Another haunt, often encountered in the

powder magazine, is so friendly and helpful that he is frequently mistaken for a tour guide.

And these are just a few of the many, many otherworldly denizens who haunt the fort.

The Fort Mifflin Paranormal Conference
June 1, 2019

This is my personal experience at the fort:

It was 8:20AM as I entered the driveway to the fort, having been fueled by coffee and directed there for the past 6 hours by my GPS. The gate was closed and I was the third car in line. I didn't know that the fort was inside an Army Corps of Engineers facility and we would have to wait for someone to unlock the gate at 9AM.

I was there as a representative of P.I.P.P. (Pennsylvania Investigators of Paranormal Phenomena) and to sell my books at the 2019 Fort Mifflin Paranormal Expo, sponsored by Haunted Explorations Events as a fundraising effort for the preservation of the fort.

Those untold number of coffees that I had consumed during the wee hours to maintain my wakefulness announced their presence through an insistent bladder. Luckily for me, there was an overgrown copse of trees to the right of the driveway that was strategically-placed in such as way as to screen me from any disapproving eyes. So I wended my way through the waist high weeds until I found a spot that provided that privacy I was seeking.

Oh, did I mention that it was a quite warm day and I dressed for it wearing shorts and sandals?

Well, while standing in the verdant undergrowth I felt the unmistakable prickle of stinging nettles on my shins.

That's how my day began...

But it got better. Within 45 minutes I was comfortably sitting under my ten by ten canopy sipping iced tea and enjoying the morning. The fort is now located at the eastern end of Philadelphia International Airport Runway 27, the favored one for landing jets. So, about every three minutes all day long we were treated to the sounds of jet engines provided by the landing planes passing about eighty feet over our heads. After an hour of this, I no longer even noticed the landing planes as I grew used to their sound.

And the day progressed just like the well-organized event promised. A constant inflow of attendees to tour the haunted fort as well as to learn its history provided a steady stream of people at my location. The speakers and presenters were all interesting and well-prepared. I met a lot of well-informed people and exchanged experiences with them. All-in-all it was a great conference.

Meeting a Pair of Spectres at the Fort.

Even though I was well aware of the fort's reputation as an intensely haunted location, I did not expect to have any experiences of my own while there for a couple of reasons.

First, it was a conference attended by many people and it has been my experience that large numbers of people tend to keep ghosts out of sight. It's as though they don't particularly care for crowds of people invading their private space. Pretty much the same way you or I would feel if uninvited people were invading our own personal space such at our homes, places of work, etc.

Second, I was attending the event as a vendor, not a paranormal investigator, and was completely unprepared to do an investigation of any sort. I didn't even have a digital recorder with me!

That's a mistake I'll never make again.

So I was caught unawares and was amazed with what happened.

It was a bit later in the day, around 2PM, when another paranormal investigator approached me and said, "Hey Ed, wanna see something out of the normal?"

Of course I replied in the affirmative and so he led me to the huge wooden gate that passes through the earthen bank that surrounds the fort and is the only entrance to it. Just inside the gate is a short passageway flanked by two rooms, each measuring about 12 feet by 12 feet. The rooms are bare with the exception of a fireplace and mantel made of stone and brick and enclosed by walls of stone. When he fort was operational these rooms were probably used by the gate guards on duty there. Today, they are empty, with not even a chair for someone to rest in.

My friend directed me to the room which is on the left as you enter the fort and I walked in.

Inside, I had the most intense paranormal encounter of the season for me. I could observe a glowing fire in the cold fireplace with flames lightly licking above the small pile of fuel therein. I approached the fireplace and put my hands out but felt absolutely no warmth from the fire. I backed away from the fireplace, looked around and, to my utter surprise, saw movement in the alcove directly to the right of the fireplace.

The shades of two men stood in that corner face to face their profiles exposed to me as they quietly conversed about something of importance to them. The were approximately five- foot six to five-foot eight in height and slight of build. I say "shades" because they appeared as shadows and were visible as dark outlines. One of them appeared to have his elbow resting on the mantel as he listened to the other. I heard unintelligible whispers between the two men and have no idea what topic they were discussing.

I turned away to inform my companion what I had seen and, when I turned back, the apparitions were gone. And, as I looked upon the fireplace, the fire within, it slowly diminished and faded from sight.

I was overwhelmed, excited, and babbled what I had seen to my friend. He simply smiled in response to my reaction and said, "This kind of s**t happens all the time here."

THE POE QUILT

**University of Pittsburgh
Cathedral of Learning
Early American Nationality Room
4500 Fifth Ave
Pittsburgh, PA 15213**

In 1926, University of Pittsburgh Chancellor John Bowman instituted the concept of Nationality Rooms to involve the diverse ethnic communities of Pittsburgh in making the inside of the Cathedral of

Leaning as imposing and spiritually impressive as the outside of that 42 story Gothic masterpiece soaring into the sky over the Oakland section of the city.

Under the direction of Ruth Crawford Mitchell, nationality groups were challenged to design and construct a classroom representative of that group's national heritage and history while, at the same time, preserving the room's practical purpose of being a place of educational instruction.

The first four rooms that were constructed in this manner were the Scottish, German, Russian, and Swedish rooms which all took nearly a decade to complete and were opened on 1938. This is an on-going project and the newest addition, the Philippine Room, was dedicated in 2019.

A self-guided audio tour of the rooms is available for a nominal charge in weekends and other times when classes aren't in session.

All-in-all there are currently 31 Nationality Rooms in operation with all but two of them also serving as operational classrooms. We are concerned with one of those two rooms, the Early American Room, the only one dedicated to our own national heritage.

Here, you are exposed to a 17th century New England style combination living room and kitchen intended to portray the harsh starkness of life in the fledgling colonies of the United States during the 1650s. Everything is 100% authentic, the result of such meticulous searches that even the chandeliers are equipped with special hinge clasps to facilitate lighting the candles on them.

A small closet between the blackboard and the 9-foot fireplace made of 200 year old bricks has a secret panel that swings open when the concealed latch is discovered. It reveals a secret staircase leading up to the upper loft that is furnished as a 19th century bedroom with a four poster rope sprung bed and a small cradle. These items were once the property of Ethelbert Nevin, an internationally known composer and pianist who attended Western University which was the forerunner of the University of Pittsburgh.

That four poster bed is adorned with the hand-made wedding quilt made by Martha Jan Poe on he occasion of her wedding to Waitman Worthington McDaniel. Mrs. Poe-McDaniel is the grandmother of the director of the Nationality Rooms Program, Maxine Bruhns as well as a relative of Edgar Allen Poe.

And now, these many years after Mrs. Poe-McDaniel's departure from this earthly plane, she seems to have developed an attachment to and an affection for that bedroom. She is considered to be he one responsible for turning down that quilt and covers and leaving a mussed-up pillow on the bed

135

after spending he night under the covers. This happens despite the efforts of staff to keep the quilt and bed covers in a state of neatness and order. Martha Jane is also presumed to be the one who rocks the cradle adjacent to the bed to soothe the unheard cries of a fretting baby within it. Both the rocking cradle and the rearrangement of the bed clothes has been witnessed by many visitors to the room.

Director Bruhns has witnessed this activity first hand as well as seeing other of her own personal belongings moving unaided in the bedroom. All she asks is that visitors to the Early American Room remain quiet and respectful should her grandmother decide to grace them with her presence.

AN ELEVATOR TO THE PAST

Gettysburg College
300 North Washington Street
Gettysburg, PA

In 1832, just 6 years after the opening of the Lutheran Seminary one half mile away, the Gettysburg College was founded at the insistence of the same man who founded the seminary, Thaddeus Stevens. It was founded by Samuel Simon Shmucker as a sister school to the seminary.

The first building on the land that Mr. Stevens provided for the college was known as Pennsylvania Hall since the college's name at that time was the Pennsylvania College of Pennsylvania. Take a stroll along the tree-lined lanes that criss-cross the greenery of the campus of the well-respected college today and enjoy the peace and tranquility that pervades the area. It is a sharp contrast to the rocky beginnings of the school's first three decades. During that time financial difficulties abounded. The wholesale departure of students from the seceding southern states nearly caused it to close its doors in 1861.

Then, on July 1, 1863 Union and Confederate forces met under a cloudy 76 degree day to begin a monumental battle that started a mere half mile away and surged in like a tidal wave overtaking the college and its surroundings for three days with soldiers fighting for control of the town.

During that battle that saw 33,000 men wounded, every available place was pressed into service to care for those men and Gettysburg College was no different. The basement of Pennsylvania Hall was quickly turned into a field hospital where both Union and Confederate soldiers were cared for, often side-by-side.

Why, you may ask, were the amputations, bandaging, and wound-cleansing operations carried out in a dimly lit basement when the building had so many other floors that were well-equipped with windows to allow light of the day to shine in? It was for practical reasons. You see, the battle raged on all around he building and neither bullets nor cannon balls held any respect for the usage of the building and they frequently flew through the upper floors.

On July 4, 1863 when the Confederates slogged southward, retreating to Virginia in a driving rain through mud and swollen streams, those wounded still lie behind, dotting the battlefield and its surroundings with their broken bodies. And the field hospital at Pennsylvania Hall still carried out its grisly duties.

While this traumatic chain of events was never forgotten, times change, generations pass, and people move on. Likewise, the college moved forward developing into a bastion of higher education that included Nobel Laureates, presidents and presidential candidates among its trustees and graduates.

Pennsylvania Hall moved into the 20th, then the 21st century and has been updated many times, outfitted with the latest in modern conveniences such as heating, air conditioning, WiFi, and a haunted time travel elevator.

Time travel elevator? Where did that come from? Haunted? W hat's that about?

Within the building is an innocuous self-service elevator just like hundreds of others that we encounter in buildings everywhere. And it is used by countless visitors to the building who need to travel from floor to floor carrying out their daily business. Most of them have no idea that they are riding on a haunted elevator.

However... Every once in a while...

More than one person has punched the button inside the elevator to be taken to an appointment on one of the floors only to find themselves transported down. Down to the basement where the field hospital was located.

When the doors silently glide open, a scene of carnage is revealed. For, not only have they been transported *down,* they have been transported *back.* Back to those horrible days during the summer of 1863.

They feel, rather than hear the screams and whimpers of wounded and dying young men having limbs amputated with neither the benefit of anesthetic nor antiseptic in the revealed silent tableau. And they see. They are confronted with a crowded area crammed with patients and doctors covered in blood-spattered clothing. Then. just as the elevator doors begin to swish closed, at least one of these people had a specter make eye contact with him, almost as though he was pleading for help.

Staring at the now-closed door of the elevator one student of the college punched the "Open Door" button time-after-time until the door opened once more only to reveal the undisturbed basement of the 21st century.

Needless to say, a number of staff, administrators, and students prefer to spend the extra few minutes that its takes to utilize the stairway, rather than chance another of these unsettling encounters.

RESERVED THEATER SEATS

Oyster Mill Playhouse
1001 Oyster Mill Road
Camp Hill, PA

After a number of years bouncing around, the Metropolitan Repertory Company found a permanent home at the former grist mill once known as the Eyster Grist Mill that had evolved into a general store, dance hall, and finally a storage facility for plumbing supplies. The MetRep Co. opened their first season in the newly renovated building they dubbed The Oyster Mill Playhouse in 1988 with a production of *Barefoot In The Park*. The rest, as they say, is history. As of this writing the

Playhouse is celebrating 43 years of successful, acclaimed, and professionally-done theater.

Of course, during these 4 decades of readings, run-throughs, off-book rehearsals and final productions the theater and the theater company have picked up an untold number of fans. Theater fans can be a bit quirky, often wanting to see the stage from the same vantage point time after time.

For some reason or other, playhouses and theaters tend to accumulate more than their fair share of spirits and the activity that they bring with them. The Oyster Mill Playhouse is no different and at least five spirits are known to frequent the building.

One is a little flaxen haired girl in a blue dress who likes to hang out around the costume racks.

Two others are of men who seem to be accompanied with a sinister feeling. One is presumed to be the spirit of a man who died there in an accident as a mill worker when the building was operated as a grist mill. The other has a mysterious past. These two have been blamed for pictures falling from the walls, lights turning on and off randomly, and indecipherable voices.

The last two are thought to be the original husband and wife who owned the property way back when it was a farm. They have become the theater's most ardent fans and seldom miss a show.

They have claimed two seats as their own: the top right and top left seat in the last row.

When someone else decides to use one of those seats for a vantage point during rehearsals or auditions, the couple gently, but insistently make their displeasure known. At least three people have learned not sit one one of these haunted seats. For, when they did so, one of the ghosts asked the squatter to move by administering a sharp tap to the head. This tap was repeated until the seat was surrendered to its original owner. Then either the farmer or his wife could peacefully settle into their seat to enjoy the performance.

ENGAGEMENT RING OF DEATH

Mercyhurst College
501 East 38th Street
Erie, PA 16546

Mercyhurst College is a small Catholic liberal arts university offering degrees in a diverse number of majors. It was founded in m1926 by the Sisters of Mercy and received its charter from the Commonwealth of Pennsylvania in 1928. From its beginning it was an all girls school until 1969 when it became coed.

As is often the case with colleges, there is a plethora of hauntings to choose from when visiting the campus with spirits inhabiting Old Main and

Egan Halls ranging from phantom musicians at the piano keyboard to, "Nora," a vengeful shade looking to right a wrong one of her relatives had committed. And don't forget the deceased nun whose body was placed in a coffin for viewing, only to get up during the night and walk away from that coffin disappearing into who-knows-where, leaving behind only her footprints.

Finally, there is "the ring."

According to campus lore, a young lady watched her lover go off to join the ranks of servicemen during World War II, vowing to wait for his return when they would be joined in wedded bliss. To seal their betrothal, he gave her an engagement ring. After the tearful farewell at the Union Station where he boarded the train that took him to Basic Training, she gathered her emotions, returned home, and waited for his return. And waited.

The war progressed, the Allies landed at Normandy on June 6, 1944 and the push was on to capture Germany and Berlin.

Then one day, she received the worst news imaginable – her fiance was reported, "Missing in Action," and, "presumed dead." Just looking at that ring on her finger that was a symbol of their love was too much for her. She knew that she could never love another man as much as she did her lost lover and so she joined the Sisters of Mercy becoming a Bride of Christ and pledging her life to Him.

She removed the ring her soldier boy had given her and placed on the finger of a statue of the Baby Jesus where it lay untouched.

The war eventually ended and, one day, to her shock, her very own soldier who was lost and presumed dead returned to claim his bride. He hadn't been killed in action after all, he had been taken prisoner and was freed when the Allies overtook the POW camp where he had been held.

But it was too late. She was a Bride of Jesus and her faith wouldn't allow her to leave the sisterhood to marry a man. And her ability to think clearly eroded until she found herself in the depths of despair and unable to resolve the situation. She saw suicide as the only way out and took her own life by hanging herself within the confines of Old Main, leaving her engagement ring where it lie untouched on the statue.

The first person to suffer from the now cursed ring was a young engaged student who was expecting a visit from the man who had pledged her his love. She took the ring from the finger of the Baby Jesus' statue and placed it on her "third finger, left hand," to wear when her fiance arrived. But he never arrived, having been killed in a disastrous freak automobile accident.

College lore has it that, anyone who has touched the ring ever since has come to a premature death within 5 years of doing so. It is reported that college administrators had even taken the action of removing the ring and putting it away for safekeeping (And to protect those who would defy the curse by touching it). Nevertheless, in spite of their efforts, it still would turn up, encircling the finger of the statue of Baby Jesus.

Nobody seems to know the location of the ring today, but the apparition of a nun in Old Main and Egan Hall is presumed to be that of the young nun who hanged herself there, possible joining in he hunt for her now missing ring.

THE MAGIC TREE

**Hamilton Street
Allentown, PA**

Can a living thing like a tree be haunted?

Busy Hamilton Street bisects Downtown Allentown and seems to have become a magnet for otherworldly activity over the years. The spirit of a young lady thought to have been killed in an automobile-pedestrian accident wanders the street near the present day Pennsylvania Power and Light Plaza where she met her end those many years ago.

Another, more apocryphal story has grown up along that Street in more recent years, It is of the "Magic Tree" of Hamilton Street that appears to be haunted in its own right. It "has been reported" that people get strange and eerie vibes in the vicinity of this tree and "strange lights" abound in its vicinity. One person has said that a picture taken of the tree has an image of a face in it.

Although I have met many people who are aware of the story of the magic tree of Hamilton Street, I have not been able to find anyone with first-hand knowledge nor have I been able to locate the exact location of the tree in the story. There are many trees along this thoroughfare.

Fact, folklore or fantasy? I just don't know.

THE HAUNTED HEATING DUCT

Irondale Inn
100 Irondale Rd.
Bloomsburg, PA

The Irondale Inn was a wonderfully appointed B & B in Bloomsburg, formed from a family home that was constructed in 1838. It saw use as a home and a way station on the underground railroad before being transformed into a B & B. The many people who stayed there over the years showered it with praise and accolades. And now ... now it is gone, closed permanently, leaving the hundreds of people who loved staying there with only their memories of good times, good service, and good food.

And perhaps memories of its ethereal residents who liked to dwell in and haunt the old cast iron heating duct.

One of the spirits was that of an elderly lady who took it upon herself to close doors behind guests when they inadvertently left them open. It brings back memories of my own dear mother admonishing me to close doors behind me and reminding me, "We aren't paying to heat the entire neighborhood." She also liked to roam the halls inside the building and was frequently seen. Guests of the B & B often reported seeing objects defying gravity by hovering in mid-air over the staircase landing. Late nights sometimes had the solitude and silenced of the building interrupted with the clatter of pans in the kitchen, accompanied by the movement of unseen beings there as well.

For some reason or another, the spirits of the Irondale Inn retreated to the safety of the cast iron heating duct that ran between the first floor and the basement when they were confronted. They could be heard rustling and speaking in low tones there. Is it possible that they may be the specters of escaped slaves who hid in that basement on their way to Canada and freedom during the mid-1800s?

With the demise of the Irondale Inn, we will probably never know.

HAUNTED AMBULANCES

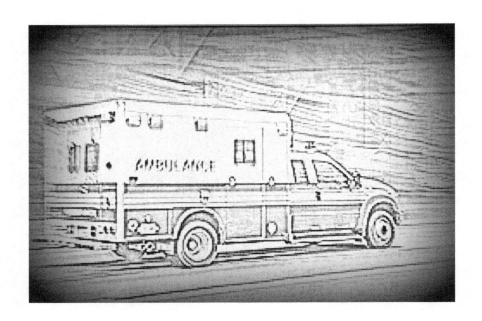

The Warminster Volunteer Ambulance Corps, Now the Central Bucks Emergency Medical Service
555 Evergreen Avenue
Warminster, PA

As I mentioned earlier, hauntings tend to gravitate to places and things that have experienced extreme emotions and traumatic events. Places like battlefields, hospitals, accident scenes, and disaster locations. Things like... ambulances. Is there any other vehicle that is host to such raw emotions, life and death decisions, joy, and despair? People are born in ambulances and people die in ambulances. So to encounter those that are haunted shouldn't such a surprise. What is surprising is that there aren't more reports of such occurrences.

Such as those at the Warminster Volunteer Ambulance Corps. The building that houses the ambulances is the site of mysterious happenings. Doors open on their own with no earthly human help. Motion detecting light switches activate and turn on lights when nobody is is present to trigger their motion sensing devices.

But that's the building, it's the ambulances that concern us. People who enter the parking bay inside the building where the ambulances are kept have heard the anguished moans of injured or sick patients coming from the ambulances when there is actually nobody in the back of the vehicles. As if that weren't enough, those who have looked in the windows to find the origin of those moans have been confronted by faces of anguished patients in the back of the ambulances. Perhaps they are shades of people being transported who didn't make it to the hospital alive.

As of Spring, 2017, the Warminster Volunteer Ambulance Corps, founded in 1960, is no more. After 57 years of saving lives, it fell upon financial hard times because those patients whose lives were saved pocketed the insurance checks that were intended to pay for their life-saving trip. The Central

Bucks County EMS replaced the Volunteer Corps and now continues saving lives from the same building that used to house the Volunteer Corps. As of this writing I am unaware as to whether or not the spirits have stayed on or if they too, have gone the way of the Warminster Volunteer Ambulance Corps.

ANNE'S ROCK

Colwyn, PA

Colwyn is a small residential borough of 2,500 or so people crammed into a 1/4 square mile area just southwest of Philadelphia. It is defined to the west by Darby Creek and to the east by Cobbs Creek.

Located along the bank of Cobbs Creek is a large boulder known as Anne's Rock. The megalith was left behind there when the glaciers of the last ice age retreated some 15,000 to 20,000 years ago. One side of the rock has an image burned into one side, the outline of which is assumed to be that of a young woman.

Local Lore has it that a Lenape Native American Princess named Anne fell in love with a white settler and the pair of lovers would secretly meet at various locations in the area. They had to meet in secret because her father, the chief of the local tribe, was adamantly against what he considered a doomed relationship. One of their favorite places to meet was at the huge rock that provided a beautiful overlook at Cobbs Creek.

Legend has it that, at one of those meetings, her father followed and saw her awaiting the arrival of her love at the rock. Here's where the story gets a bit murky.

One version tells us that, when Anne saw the approach of her father, she leaped from the rock into the stream below, either dying from injuries received as a result of the fall, or drowning in the rushing waters of Cobbs Creek.

The other version accounts for he image burned into one side of the rock. It says that, upon her father's approach, lightning struck the rock, obliterating her earthly substance and burning its image into the rock.

She is still there at the rock, patiently waiting for her love to arrive so that they may be together once and forever.

Persons who visit the rock report the smell of herbs and a choking sensation. *(Perhaps it is as a result of actually smoking the herbs. That'll cause a coughing fit from time to time. Not that I'm speaking from personal experience, mind you.)*

A paranormal investigation was conducted at the rock in the fall of 2018 by the Tri-county Paranormal Society. Using a Spirit Box, the group was able to collect a number of EVPs at the site. Some of the findings indicate that the spirit who haunts the area is *not* named Anne, is *not* Native American and may not even be female.

It is possible that the spirit the Tri-county Paranormal Society contacted may have been that of Anne's lover and that for, some reason or other, Anne wasn't present at that time.

Or, it may be that Anne is a fabrication of local lore and doesn't actually exist.

THE HAT

Brinton Lodge
1808 Schuylkill Rd.
Douglasville, PA 19518

Originally a farmhouse built in the 1700s, the Brinton Lodge has grown exponentially during the 300-plus years of its existence into the magnificent 28 room mansion that it is today. It has sat here during all these years watching as the country developed. At one time, the Schuylkill River Canal bisected its property carrying people and products to and from western destinations. Residents have included farmers, munitions manufacturers, and people escaping slavery on their way to freedom. It was an exclusive gentleman's club during the Prohibition and until recently, an excellent restaurant. Now it is home to a craft brewery and brewpub called the Hidden River Brewing Company.

Of course, having such a rich, varied and extensive history, it has picked up its share of haunts along the way. The occupants of some historic buildings tend to downplay reports of paranormal activity. Not these people. They revel in it, even offering monthly ghost tours and opening the doors for private investigations as well.

Some of the ghosts you may encounter whilst quaffing a craft beer and enjoying some of its farm-to-table menu items, include "the Dark Shadow" who has been frequently sighted by patrons as well as employees for nearly 40 years in all areas of the mansion. Five other spirits have been identified there as well. Other things reported are phantom footsteps, moving objects, and a plethora of apparitions. Small wonder then, that it is considered one of the top 10 haunted houses in Pennsylvania.

When the lodge was the home of the Covetta's Brinton Lodge Restaurant, there was the oft repeated incident of the haunted hat. It wasn't anything special, just a hat. Then, one day it found its home on the mantel of the fireplace in the restaurant. For a while nobody noticed its penchant for reappearing on that mantel, always assuming that one of the other employees of the restaurant returned it there after it had been moved to a nearby shelf.

Conversations usually went something like this:

"Did you move the hat back onto the mantel?"

"No, I thought you did it."

"OK ..."

Finally, the hat was taken away and put into a closet one day at closing time. The next morning, the employee who opened the restaurant noticed it on the mantel once again. That night, they locked the closet with the hat inside. The very next morning it was back on the mantel and the closet was still locked.

Nobody knows what specter insisted on placing the hat back on the mantel, likewise nobody knows why.

THE HAUNTED CAROUSEL

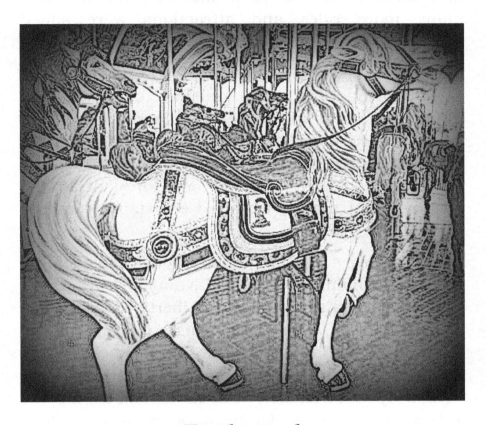

Hersheypark
100 Hersheypark Drive
Hershey, PA 17033

Hersheypark is a world class family oriented theme park located in Hershey, PA. It was built in 1906 and opened to the public as a leisure park including a baseball field surrounded by a track. The first amusement park ride was added in 1908, a Herschel Spillman carousel. And the start of the amusement park was set in motion. Over the years many more rides and attractions were added resulting in the great vacation destination that is Hersheypark today.

Shortly after the original carousel was purchased and put into operation in 1908, the need for a larger one became evident. So, in 1913 another, larger carousel was purchased from the William H Dentzel Company and brought to the park where it thrilled kids and entertained parents until 1944.

In turn it was replaced by Philadelphia Toboggan Company Carrousel Number 47 that was built in 1919 and installed at Liberty Heights Park near Baltimore, Maryland, where it stayed until 1929. During that year of the famed stock market crash that started the Great Depression it was bought by and installed at Enna Jettick Park some 250 miles north of Hersheypark in Auburn, New York. For fifteen years it was enjoyed by the families visiting the Finger Lakes Region of the Empire State. Then, in 1944, it was purchased by Hersheypark and installed there in 1945. Carrousel Number 47 has been merrily going around ever since. The Dentzel Carousel? It was sold to Kotts Berry Farm in California where it still is in operation to this very day.

Today, Carrousel #47 is in its third location. It

was originally housed in a pavilion alongside Spring Creek where it stayed for 26 years. Then, during thew winter of 1971, it was moved to a new area of the park appropriately named Carousel Circle where its 66 prancing horses, 42 of which go up and down, raced in an endless circle.

In 2018 plans to relocate it once more to a place more fitting for the centenarian at the park's entrance was announced.

Now, all this history is interesting, but what does it have to do with this book. Simple – the carousel is haunted.

Late at night after all the amusement park visitors have gone home and all the rides are darkened, the overnight maintenance force comes out to get everything ready for the next day's operation.

As they sweep the pathways, restock the games and souvenir stands, imagine how the worker feels when he or she hears the gentle whine of electric motors as the carousel, unaided by any earthly input, comes slowly to life. One by one, the strings of lights flicker and brighten. Slowly at first, then faster as it comes up to speed, the hand-carved horses start to go up and down as the platform where they reside revolves. And all this is accompanied by the eerily quiet at first, then louder and louder musical strains of the antique Wurlitzer

Band Organ.

And all this is under the control of a phantom that has only been seen once, to my knowledge. A security guard who encountered the spectral activity at the carousel shut off the lights one evening after they had come on spontaneously. As soon as he had turned them off, they came on again.

It was at that point he observed a shadow figure at the controls of the ride. As he approached the location where he had seen the shadow figure, it faded and disappeared.

CURSED CLOCK OF THE FAYETTE COUNTY COURTHOUSE

North & West Faces

South & East Faces

Photos Were Both Taken Within 5 Minutes of One Another

Uniontown, PA

From his honored perch high atop the courthouse of the county bearing his name, the Marquis de Lafayette has the best vantage point in Uniontown, PA. And he has enjoyed the panorama of the valley in this manner since March of 1847. From 188 feet above Main Street he had the best view of anyone of the old county prison jail yard where executions by hanging were carried out until 1914.

So, it is probable that his stern visage was cast upon an unfortunate soul who had been condemned to die. He was scheduled to to hang from his neck until dead on the gallows at the Fayette County Prison in Uniontown, PA as the courthouse bell tolled the noon hour. He was definitely guilty of the crime for which he had been sentenced. The sentence was true and just. He was aware of his guilt and had no argument with any of the proceedings. Except one.

10 minutes before the scheduled execution the prisoner was led up the creaking steps of the gallows located in the jail yard. His feet were placed on the trap door whose opening would end his stay on this mortal coil. The noose was placed around his neck and snugged, but not too tight. He could still speak.

He still had 5 minutes to go before his scheduled end, but the hangman, who possibly had a more pressing engagement elsewhere wanted to speed things up. He asked the hapless condemned man if he has any final words before the trap was sprung.

The prisoner looked up, not to God in heaven, but to the courthouse clock looming over him which indicated that he still had 5 minutes to go. He realized that he still had 5 minutes to go and that he was about to be cheated out of his last 5 minutes of life. He was speechless with rage.

The hangman mistaking his mute rage for a refusal to speak, placed the hood over his head and the executioner's hand reached for the lever. He only had short seconds to make his final statement. What to say?

Did he apologize for his crime that brought him to this terminus? No. Did he curse the judge, jury, and police? No. Did he beg for his miserable life, such as it was? No.

No indeed. Instead of any of those, his voice muffled by the hood, cursed the clock that showed him that he was being executed 5 minutes early. He cursed it to forever run 5 minutes slow to atone for those 5 minutes of life stolen from him by the impatient executioner.

>*<

In a slightly different version, the prisoner's last statement curses the clock to always show a different time on its four faces.

In any case, the four faces of time on the courthouse tower have never agreed as to the proper time of day, and still do not.

ANNA'S WEDDING GOWN

Baker Mansion
Altoona, PA

Elias Baker was a self-made man whose Allaghany Furnace produced enough iron on a daily basis to make him millions of dollars. So, in 1844 the first brick was laid in what would be the biggest, most opulent, and most expensive mansion in the Altoona region. It took five years to build, using only the best products available and decorated in such a way as to make a pharaoh proud.

You see, Elias loved his family and, while it is difficult to imagine people actually living a day-to-day existence among all this splendor, it is because Elias Baker would stand for nothing less than the absolute finest in all things for his family.

Of all his family Elias loved his daughter Anna more than anyone else in the world. She was the apple of his eye, nothing was too good for his little princess.

Time passed and Anna grew into a beautiful young woman. One day she met the love of her life, a young man from the area. With some trepidation, young Anna went to her father and explained that she had fallen in love and wanted his blessing so that she could marry her young beau. Elias asked who the lucky young man was, and when Anna told him, he was outraged to the point of apoplexy, It seemed that Anna's young man was a mere penniless worker, a commoner. There was no way Elias could countenance a union between his little princess and an unwashed plebeian. He forbade the union and that was that.

Even though she thought it unfair, she obeyed her father's demands and broke it off with her suitor. However, knowing that she would never meet anyone who could replace that young man in her heart, she never formed any relationship with another man for the balance of her life. She died a spinster in 1914.

But, before she had asked her dad's permission, she did a few things. You see, being her daddy's princess and never having him say no to her during her entire young life, she was convinced that he would surely give her marriage his blessing. So, before she even asked for his permission to marry, she had had crafted for her a wedding dress that could only exist in a princess' dreams. For only a royal family could afford such a garment. It was never to be worn by its intended. The daughter of another wealthy nearby family did wear it for *her* wedding. Elizabeth Bell is rumored to have mocked Anna for never marrying while walking down the aisle in Anna's dress.

Anna was finally got to wear her wedding dress, just not in her lifetime. Visitors and museum staff alike have witnessed the gown turning first this way, then that in its display case behind protective glass. Many explanations have been given for this seemingly inexplicable event ranging from loose floorboards to stray breezes. Of course there are no loose floorboards in the fortress-constructed mansion and likewise, there are no breezes inside the sealed glass case. It appears that it is Anna herself trying on the dress and preening in it, trying to decide which view is most flattering. In death, she has accomplished what she couldn't in life – wearing her wedding gown.

SOUNDS OF MASSACRE

The Fulton Opera House
12 North Prince Street
Lancaster, PA

When the Fulton Opera House is supposedly empty, workers hear unearthly screams. And no, these sounds are not coming from the throats of would-be opera singers.

You see, it isn't so much that the building is haunted (though it is) as that the very ground it is built on is haunted.

The Fulton Opera House has stood on this spot for over 150 years and has had its boards trod upon by the greatest of the great in the history of entertainment. Theatrical giants have appeared here. The royal family of the stage, the Barrymores, acted here, as did Sarah Bernhardt (known as the Divine Sarah), Al Jolson, W. C. Fields, Alfred Lunt, and Irene Dunne. A bushy-browed, white-haired gentleman with the stage name of Mark Twain offered up his pithy, homespun, view of Americana from this very stage. Edward and John Wilkes Booth were both famous tragedians who appeared here long before John's fame turned to infamy. The building's namesake, Robert Fulton, inventor of the steamship, watches over all from his statue in a niche three floors above Prince Street.

This Grand Old Lady, the oldest continuously operating theater in the country, is one of only eight named National Historic Landmarks.

Long before theatergoers were held in thrall, this spot was home to a more captive audience. The original Lancaster County Jail sat on this spot and held a full house of prisoners in chains and cells.

The early 1760s were a turbulent and dangerous time in Pennsylvania. The French and

Indian War had just come to a close, and the victorious British were heavy-handed in enforcing their victory. Chief Pontiac of the Ottawa Tribe, a respected statesman, was able to form a loose-knit confederation of tribes of the Ohio, Illinois, and Great Lakes regions. Their intended purpose was to drive both the British soldiers and the British settlers out of the ancestral lands that had been stolen from them. This uprising came to be known as Pontiac's War and was noteworthy for its ruthlessness and treachery. Scalping, an atrocity introduced by the British, became commonplace, as did the massacre of prisoners and bystanders and the targeting of civilians. The most infamous of these was when British officers at Fort Pitt provided Indians with blankets infected with smallpox in the hope that Indian families would be killed by the disease.

On top of everything else, the Governor of Pennsylvania, James Hamilton, refused to send troops to the rescue of the frontier people. This caused the formation of impromptu and informally led militia groups throughout the commonwealth. In no time, instead of protecting citizens, these groups became nothing more than murderers dedicated to the eradication of Native Americans from Pennsylvania.

One of the most vicious of these groups was known as the Paxton (or Paxtang) Boys. It was composed of over 200 men recruited by Reverend John Elder of Paxton Presbyterian Church near Harrisburg. This group quickly disintegrated from a protective unit to one devoted to the killing of all Indians. Peaceful or warlike, it made no difference to them. Maybe this is the origin of that racist saying, "The only good Indian is a dead Indian."

The Reverend Elder was fixated on eliminating a native who went by the name of Captain Bull. He was certainly a bane to peaceful existence and was responsible for the deaths of numerous settlers in Berks County. The Reverend set the rangers, as the Paxton Boys liked to call themselves, on the trail of Captain Bull. These self-styled rangers claimed that they had traced a number of Captain Bull's warriors to a place known as Conestoga. The Susquehannock Indians who lived in Conestoga were a peaceful community and they had been converted to Christianity by Moravian missionaries.

In the meantime, John Penn had replaced James Hamilton as Governor of Pennsylvania. The Reverend Elder immediately petitioned him, asking that all the Indians be removed from Pennsylvania. The Governor wrote back: "The faith of this government is pledged for their protection. I cannot remove them without adequate cause." This wasn't what the good reverend wanted to hear, so he sent the Paxton Boys out to do what the government wouldn't.

At dawn on a frigid December morning, the Indians in the little Conestoga village awakened to the sound of fifty armed men heading their way. Knowing what was likely to come, they ran out of their homes wearing only the clothes on their backs, carrying the younger children. Old people stumbled and fell in the snow.

The so-called rangers held Indians in such contempt that they felt that it would be wasteful to spend bullets and powder on them. They rode the fleeing people down and clubbed them to death. One small boy was swept up by a ranger and had his head bashed against a tree.

Fourteen of the villagers escaped and sought protection from their Moravian benefactors. Some of the survivors continued on to Philadelphia. Those old people and children who couldn't travel fast sought protection from the sheriff in Lancaster. The sheriff housed them in the jail, locking the cells for their protection. Surely this old fortress could prevent break-ins as well as breakouts.

Captain Lazarus Stewart of the Paxton Boys somehow learned that Captain Bull was among the survivors in the Lancaster jail. He convinced his men to ride on to Lancaster so that they could demand that Captain Bull be released into their custody, ostensibly to go to Carlisle for trial.

They found no one of authority at the jail.

However, the jailer, before his rapid departure, had left the keys lying in plain sight on his desk.

The Paxton Boys entered the cells where the Indians had taken refuge and slaughtered them. The old people threw their bodies over the children to protect them, but to no avail. Their attempts to defend the children only fed the vigilantes' blood lust. Every man, woman, and child in those cells was beaten, stomped, slashed, and hacked to death. There were no survivors. The infamous Captain Bull, who was the start of much of the antagonism in the area, died in the slaughter.

The final few survivors made it to Philadelphia and sought sanctuary. When the Paxton Boys trailed them, a contingent of armed citizens led by Benjamin Franklin refused them entry. Those last survivors lived out their years in Philadelphia. When they died, so did the Susquehannock Indian tribe. The Reverend Elder got his wish.

That jail was razed and the Fulton Opera House was built on the blood-soaked grounds. The only remains from that terrible day, December 27, 1763, are the old gates of the prison in the basement and a simple plaque on the wall listing the names of the victims.

The unearthly screams that workers hear may be coming from the mouths of children and old folk in their dying throes. In any case they always seem to come from behind they old gates of the prison that have been discarded in the basement of the opera house. Few people can spend any extended time in the basement of that historic building. They feel the presence of the murdered Indians and an unnerving sense of silent watching, watching, watching . . .

THE DART GUN

1806 Antiques
Route 30
Jennerstown, PA

On October 28, 2019, members of the Pennsylvania Investigators of Paranormal Phenomena conducted a paranormal investigation at this location. During the course of this investigation, numerous spirits were encountered. The full story of the investigation will be told in a different publication as this one deals particularly with haunted objects. In another place in this book, I have told the story of the haunted mirror in the second floor powder room.

Now I will tell you about a second haunted object found in this wonderful antique emporium.

During the course of our investigation, one team started in the basement while the second team started on the first floor. These were the two psychics on the investigation: Beverly LaGorga and Kat Henderson. They were kept separated so they wouldn't influence one another with their individual findings. It's just one of the safeguards we practice to maintain a system of checks and balances throughout our investigations.

Kat was accompanied by Brendan Kelemen who was equipped with a digital recorder and a video camera.

After wending their way through the first floor, they made their way to the second floor where Kat encountered the spirits of two small children who are resident haunts of the building.

The little girl's name is Sara. She passed away on the premises during a smallpox outbreak in 1861.

Attempts at finding out the little boy's name have been unsuccessful, but it is felt that he died as a result of an accident within one of the small homes located behind the main building, possibly during the early 1900s. Those small buildings are now long gone.

Of course Kat was kept unaware of the presence of the spirits of the two children and she was amazed and delighted when she encountered them in the back room on the second floor. You see, Kat has a special affinity for both children and the spirits of children. They are naturally drawn to her.

While she was crouched down speaking with the children, misty shapes appeared on the video feed just above and to the right of Kat's head. The children happily engaged Kat and even directed her to a hidden stash of their toys under a table in the far corner of he room.

> NOTE: These toys have been provided to the children by Fran, one of the owners. The sounds of the children playing with them is frequently heard by persons on the first floor. Also, the children like to play a game of hide-and-seek with Fran.
>
> It works like this: Fran gave the kids a few marbles a long time ago. The marbles disappear from where Fran put them with

the kids toys, only to turn up somewhere else, usually on the second floor. Then Fran returns the marbles to the original location under the table and the game starts anew.

After promising the kids that she would be back, Kat and Brendan left the room and worked their way upstairs to the attic. Kat had an encounter up there with a grumpy old man, examined some artifacts that caught her attention, then Brendan and she returned to the second floor to check things in what she called "The Candle Room." Beverly and I passed them on the stairs on our way to the attic. Bev encountered the grumpy old man's spirit up there as well, but called him a "Sourpuss."

One of the collection of items in the attic was displayed on an old ironing board and consisted of miscellaneous items ranging from hand tools to toys.

Without warning, our K-II meter started pinging on the ironing board, going all the way into the red zone. Beverly felt no otherworldly presence on or around the ironing board. Nevertheless, the K-II meter was going wild at the ironing board. As soon as it was withdrawn from the area of the ironing board, it settled back down to its green zone. Then, once it was brought near the ironing board again, it went into the red.

We were mystified and started removing items

one-by-one from the ironing board and placing them on a nearby table. The K-II meter had no reaction to the items on the table. Eventually, we worked our way through the motley collection to a small plastic dart gun of the type that used to be sold for about 50 cents during the 1950s. We placed it separately on the table, then moved the K-II meter to its proximity and the K-II meter went into the red again.

Again, we were perplexed and called out to the other team to come up and see what they made of the situation.

Kat and Brendan quickly responded and we told them what was happening and demonstrated how the K-II meter was reacting on the little toy dart gun.

Kat said, "I know what's going on."

So we persuaded her to include the rest of us in her circle of knowledge and she responded by saying, "I think the little boy ghost on the second floor wants to play with the dart gun and he's afraid of just taking it without permission. This is his way of asking for it."

So, after first clearing it with Fran, we removed the dart gun from its place in the attic and took it down to the second floor where Kat placed it under the table with the rest of the toys saying, "Here's your dart gun, little guy. Hope you have lots of fun with it."

At this point we placed the K-II meter next to the dart gun and it gave no reading whatsoever.

Next thing we knew, Kat was standing over to one side of the room, tears streaming down her face. Concerned, I asked her what was wrong.

Smiling through the tears, she said, "Nothing. The little boy just ran over here and wrapped his arms around my legs saying thanks."

LINCOLN'S BED

The Heinz History Center
Pittsburgh, PA

Cursed? Or Haunted? A massively carved wooden bed is on display at the Heinz History Center. It was originally one of the furnishings of the now long-gone Monongahela House, Pittsburgh's grand 300 room hotel of the 1800s.

In 1861, President-elect Abraham Lincoln stopped in Pittsburgh en route to his inauguration in Washington, DC. It was a dismal February 15 with icy rain coming down in sheets for hours. Although due in the city at 6 pm, his train was delayed for two hours because of a freight train that had broken down blocking the track. He eventually arrived in Allegheny City (Now the North Side of Pittsburgh) at 8 pm and took a carriage across the Allegheny River to Pittsburgh.

Lincoln was amazed at the size and enthusiasm of the crowds who braved the weather and thronged the streets of the city to meet him. He made the statement in the ornate lobby of he Monongahela House, "I could not help thinking, my friends, as I traveled in the rain through your crowded streets, on my way here, that if all that people were in favor of the Union, it can certainly be in no great danger – it will be preserved."

Then he spent the night in the hotel, sleeping in the very bed that is now on display at the history center. Upon his departure, hotel management decided that henceforth, the room Lincoln slept in would only be available to elite members of society, the gentility, the beautiful people.

And so it was, that room was reserved for the hoi polloi. In future years those members of the upper crust included Presidents James Garfield and William McKinley.

And what do the three presidents have in common? They all slept in that walnut bed and they were all assassinated! Lincoln in 1865, Garfield in 1881, and McKinley in 1901.

So – is the bed haunted by a vengeful spirit? Is it cursed? Or is it a mere coincidence?

THE HAUNTED BELL

Franklin and Marshall College
Lancaster, PA

In 1787, Benjamin Franklin kicked in a large amount of money to fund and found this private liberal arts institute of higher learning. So of course, it was named Franklin College. Forty nine years and 101 miles west, Marshall College, named after Supreme Court Justice John Marshall opened in Mercersburg, PA.

Then, in 1849, the two school merged with the

new school located in Lancaster and called Franklin and Marshall College.

Today it is a well respected medium sized liberal arts college with a bit over 2,400 students in a variety of majors ranging from Classical Archaeology to Women's Studies and everything in between.

Looking back over two centuries of history it would be unusual if the college didn't pick up its share of haunts and hauntings. And in this case, Franklin and Marshall is not unusual.

Many people have experienced ghostly encounters within the buildings on the rolling rural campus. These range from screams and moans to furniture moving of its own volition, doors slamming with neither human nor wind assistance, and apparitions of deceased students.

Overlooking the campus from its vantage point is the venerable old brass bell high up in the tower of Old Main was the first building built exclusively for Franklin and Marshall and was originally used to house the students of the newly-merged schools. The bell was rung to announce the start and end of classes for the day as well as the changing of classes during the day.

This practice has long since been abandoned as technology has replaced manpower to start and end classes. The last time the bell was rung on purpose was to celebrate the inauguration of a new college president in 2002.

The bell, or perhaps the spirit of a long since matriculated bell ringer, does not like being abandoned in this cavalier manner. This disagreement with college policy is demonstrated by the bell tolling at irregular times of the night on random days with no living human assistance in the matter.

On a cloudy, cold winter evening, from time-to-time an undergraduate hurrying from one point to another across campus may just wonder for whom *does* the bell toll.

Ed Kelemen

THE CAULDRON
OR

**How Mad Anthony Wayne
haunts a cemetery in Philadelphia,
a section of of US Route 322,
and the
The Watson-Curtze Mansion,
now the Erie County History Center,
at 356 West 6th Street
Erie, PA**

I can think of no better way to finish this book than with the story of one of my favorite denizens of the afterlife, whose experiences after death have been as eventful as those he had when still living – Anthony Wayne.

In 1892, this imposing 24-room brownstone mansion with 12 fireplaces, stained-glass windows, intricate wooden carvings and Tiffany light shades was built for Erie roofing paper magnate and inventor Harrison F. Watson who lived there with his wife and daughter until 1923. At that time, it was bought by Erie Trust Company President Fredrick Felix Curtze who resided there until his death in 1941 when the family donated it to become a museum. Today it is operated as such by the Erie County Historical Society.

Here, we are going to discuss something and someone which is apparently totally unrelated to the Watson-Curtze Mansion – General "Mad Anthony" Wayne of the American Revolution.

Anthony Wayne was a successful businessman from Eastern Pennsylvania who served in the Pennsylvania Legislature during 1784. At the outbreak of hostilities, he immediately joined the revolution by raising a regiment for the fledgling Continental Army where he rose through the ranks to Brigadier General.

There were three things that stood out about

General Wayne. First was his volatile and mercurial temper when he encountered people and things that went against his grain. Second was his cool, calculating, and brilliant manner of leading his troops in combat. And third was his devotion to those same troops.

In 1704, an Inn was constructed for travelers at what is now 625 Montgomery Avenue in Merion, PA on what would become the Philadelphia Main Line. During its existence was was known as the Wayside Inn, the Tunis Ordinary, Streepers Tavern and the William Penn Inn before changing its name forever in 1793. For that was when General Anthony Wayne and his regiment descended on the Inn for a celebration. Anthony Wayne had just led them to victory yet one more time when the odds were against them. However, this one was one that produced a treaty with the Native Americans in what was then called the Northwest Territories. Today we call that area Ohio. The celebration at the Inn went on day and night for over a week.

The Innkeeper was so impressed with the way the general allowed his men to blow off steam and celebrate that he renamed the place the General Wayne Inn. And it kept that name for over 225 years, even being placed on the List of National Historic Places. (It was also one of Edgar Allen Poe's favorite places where he would consume his favorite rabbit stew while sitting near a window that provided the needed light for him to pen some of his stories and poems, including "The Raven.") Others left their essence behind at that establishment including Hessian soldiers. Finally, it fell into disuse after the partners who owned it fell out over a love triangle that resulted in murder and jail sentences for the survivors during the 1990s. In 2005, it was purchased by the Chabad of the Main Line and converted into a synagogue and community center.

This is just one indication of his popularity. There are towns, boroughs, cities, and counties named after him in Pennsylvania, Ohio, New York, Georgia, and Tennessee.

Back to Anthony Wayne. He achieved the sobriquet of, "Mad Anthony," when one of his soldiers who General Wayne frequently used as a spy and a scout known as "Jemmy The Rover," because of his tendency to wander away from the army was apprehended by local authorities on a charge of disorderly conduct. Telling the local constabulary that General Wayne was a personal friend who would vouch for him, Jemmy, also known as "The Commodore" demanded to be set free. The constables refused, causing Jemmy to insist that a messenger be sent to General Wayne demanding his freedom.

General Anthony Wayne's famous temper flared and he responded by refusing Jemmy's requested assistance, adding that, if it happened again, he would order, "29 lashes, laid well-on," in addition to any penalty the civilian authorities would impose.

Jemmy responded with a tirade of his own saying, "Anthony is mad! He must be mad or he would help me! Mad Anthony, that's what he is! Mad Anthony Wayne!"

This humorous tale spread throughout the Continental Army campfires and was repeated by soldiers in the ranks. "Mad Anthony Wayne" had a rhythm and cadence that caught on and stuck. General Wayne's penchant for leading his troops into precarious positions only to come out triumphant reinforced his reputation as "Mad."

After the war, General Wayne settled in Georgia, serving as a representative of that state to the Second United States Congress in 1791. After some difficulty about election fraud, he was replaced by a fellow named John Milledge.

Just about that time, President George Washington recalled Wayne into the army and gave him the responsibility of quelling the Indian uprising in the Northwest Territory of the new country. It seems as though the British conveniently forgot to tell its Native American allies that the war was over. Keep in mind that the "Northwest Territory" of that time consisted of what today is Indiana, Ohio, and Western Pennsylvania.

After a couple of years of constant warfare, General Wayne ended the hostilities with the treaty of Greeneville. The following year, General Anthony Wayne contracted gout and returned to the fort at Erie to recuperate. But, unfortunately, he died of complications from the gout and was buried at the base of the flag pole at Fort Presque Isle in Northwestern Pennsylvania on December 15, 1796. The Wayne Blockhouse stands at that location today.

And that's where his saga should have ended. But such was not to be the case...

You see, Anthony Wayne had a daughter, Margretta, who thought it was shameful that her illustrious father was buried at some godforsaken place on the frontier, probably even in unhallowed ground. She felt that he deserved a proper burial within the graveyard of St. Davids Episcopal Church in Wayne, PA, now called Radnor, PA.

So, she embarked on a campaign of nagging entreaty, making Issac, her brother's, life miserable until he agreed to retrieve Dear Old Dad's body for a church service and burial in the family plot. So, off to Erie went Issac in a sulky which was a light weight two-wheeled horse dawn cart.

In 1809, 13 years after Anthony Wayne had left this mortal coil, his son caused his remains to be disinterred. Imagine his consternation when he found that, for some reason or another, decomposition hadn't taken place. Mad Anthony Wayne's remains were still mostly intact. What to do?

No problem. Doctor Wallace, who interestingly enough was the attending physician at the General's death, offered up a solution. The meat, sinews and fat would be scraped and boiled off the bones. The clean bones then would be easily transported back east for burial. And this was done with the broth, meat, and other leavings poured back into the grave where the general had been buried.

Issac then packed the bones into the trunk affixed to the sulky and set off for Philadelphia and the General's bones were then buried at the church cemetery with full ceremony.

Again, that should be where the story ends. But it doesn't...

You see, the trunk used to transport the general's bones over 400 miles from Erie to Wayne, PA had a faulty latch. At some point along the journey back to Philadelphia along the rutted, rocky, and uneven roads, the latch failed, the lid to the trunk popped open, and a number of the bones fell out along the way and were lost.

Right here, "Mad" Anthony Wayne turned into

"Angry" Anthony Wayne and, every year on his birthday, January first, he travels a length of Old US Route 322 on his war horse, in full uniform and regalia, searching for his lost bones which, by now, have probably weathered away into dust.

Here would be yet one more place for this story to end. But alas, it goes on...

Remember what happened after the carcass of General Wayne was boiled to clean the bones? The meat, broth, fat, sinews, tools, implements, and the cauldron used for that purpose were all poured back into the poor fellow's original grave and his coffin lid was placed over them.

In 1853 arsonists burned the original blockhouse where the flag pole had been marking the site of the grave. Subsequently, the whole area was levelled and the grave site was lost. Then, in 1878, a Dr, Germer of Erie investigated, found the grave, and had it opened once again. The coffin lid, some clothing, and some of Dr. Wallace's instruments were recovered, and are on display in the block house which has been built and rebuilt several times since that time. Whatever remains of the General are still in the ground under the block house, making him one of a select group. He is buried in two places nearly 400 miles apart! The disposition of the cauldron was murky at best.

End of story, right? Wrong.

Now, we come back to the Watson-Curtze Mansion after this long detour. At sometime after 1878, what has been said to be the iron cauldron used to boil the flesh and meat from the bones of General Wayne's cadaver has found its way into the collection at the mansion and is, from time-to-time put on display here. When on display it is accompanied with an explanation of its one-time use. And that would be that, except for the activity of the cauldron after hours and when it is put away into storage.

Anthony Wayne is possibly less than happy about the cavalier way his earthly remains have been treated during the last two and a quarter centuries. The cauldron emits sounds suspiciously like bones being rattled and banged inside the cauldron when the museum is closed. Then, when it is put away in a closet, its unseen contents shake on the shelf, almost falling off. I like to think the General's spirit is saying, "Here – come look what they've done to me."

ABOUT THE AUTHOR

Ed Kelemen is an author, playwright, and columnist who spends an inordinate amount of time with the Pennsylvania Investigators of Paranormal Phenomena (P.I.P.P.) as both a technician and a paranormal investigator. During the course of writing his Haunted Pennsylvania Collection, he has been involved in over 300 paranormal investigations.

Visitors are always welcome at his website at www.ekelemen.com and he can be easily contacted via email at ed@ekelemen.com.

Other Books by the Author
THE HAUNTED PENNSYLVANIA COLLECTION

 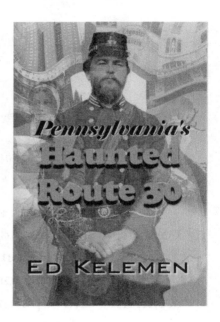

Pennsylvania's Haunted Route 22 and Pennsylvania's Haunted Route 30 are comprehensive spooky road trips along both of those highways, beginning at Point State Park in Pittsburgh and ending at haunted watering holes at the Pennsylvania-New Jersey line.

Paranormal PA is the third in the series about otherworldly activity in Pennsylvania. It concentrates on extraordinary events that happen to ordinary, everyday people, just like you and I.

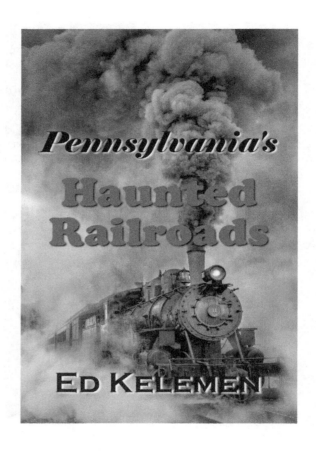

Pennsylvania's Haunted Railroads, the fourth in this series, is a mixture of history and hauntings, diesel and steam, following the design, development, and demise of the iron horses during nearly 200 years of prominence.

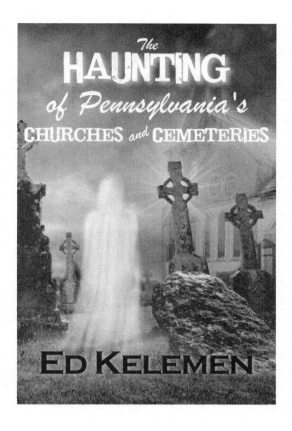

Take a trip to Pennsylvania's cemeteries. Who knows who or what you may encounter on these hallowed and sometimes not so hallowed grounds..

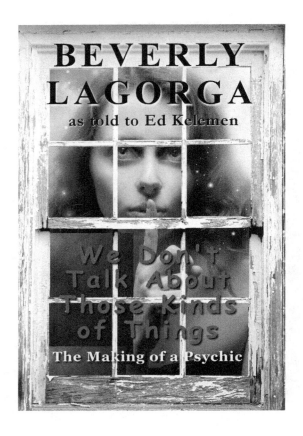

We Don't Talk About Those Kinds of Things – The Making of a Psychic is the autobiography of Beverly LaGorga who tells the story of her life beginning when she was a frightened youngster. It culminates with her development into an experienced psychic-medium. Ed feels privileged to have helped her get it into print.

Made in the USA
Middletown, DE
01 November 2023

41596529R00126